GUIDING SOULS

Dialogues on the Purpose of Life

From the Team of 'WINGS OF FIRE'

GUIDING SOULS

Dialogues on the Purpose of Life

Dr. A.P.J. Abdul Kalam

with

Arun K. Tiwari

Ocean Books Pvt. Ltd.

ISO 9001:2015 Publishers

Published by
Ocean Books (P) Ltd.
4/19 Asaf Ali Road,
New Delhi-110 002 (INDIA)
e-mail: info@oceanbooks.in

ISBN 978-81-8430-343-8
GUIDING SOULS: DIALOGUES ON THE PURPOSE OF LIFE
by Dr. A.P.J. Abdul Kalam with Arun K Tiwari

Edition
2025

Price
₹ 350.00 (Rupees Three Hundred Fifty only)

Printed at
Narula Printers, Delhi

Righteousness

Where there is righteousness in the heart,
there is beauty in character.
Where there is beauty in character,
there is harmony in the home.
Where there is harmony in the home,
there is order in the nation.
Where there is order in the nation,
there is peace in the world.

A Hymn

إِن كُلُّ نَفْسٍ لَّمَّا عَلَيْهَا حَافِظٌ ﴿٤﴾

In Kullu nafsin lamma aaleyha Hafiz

No human soul but hath a guardian over it.

Al-Tariq (The Morning-Star)
The Holy Quran (86.4)

मयि सर्वमिदं प्रोतं सूत्रे मणिगणा इव ॥

Mayi sarwa-midam protam
Sutre mani-gana iva

Everything rests upon Me,
As pearls are strung on a thread.

Text 7: Chapter VII, Line 2
The Bhagvad Gita

This book is dedicated to
all righteous people,
wherever they live on this planet.

PREFACE

IN *Ignited Minds*, a dream is narrated wherein I meet five people—Asoka, Abraham Lincoln, Mahatma Gandhi, Caliph Umar and Einstein. These five enlightened souls discuss the madness of mankind in a moonlit desert: Why is man driven by a self-destructive impulse which causes incalculable harm and suffering to humanity? The book takes off from this dream emphasising the importance of a creative thought-process that embodies the essence of a noble human being. It was released on the eve of my taking over Presidency in July 2002.

As President of the Indian Republic, I travelled across the length and breadth of my vast country and had the opportunity to interact with a wide cross-section of people, including some distinguished spiritual leaders. My awareness of the many galaxies that constitute the Universe of human thought became more extensive, and my understanding more intensive. The richness and diversity of India's social, spiritual and cultural mosaic never ceases to fill me with awe and admiration.

In a process that is akin to a seed germinating suddenly, certain spiritual guideposts appear showing the way, or the right path. I would call these spiritual guideposts *Guiding Souls*, endowed with a mission to steer human lives in the affairs of this world. Human awareness and experience is taken beyond blind faith and toil to a higher plane of spiritual certainty and purposeful effort. From a scientific perspective, the inner being of a person can be seen as an amorphous collection of thoughts, images, emotions, sensations, dreams, insights and inspiration. Add a little sensitivity to the relation between metaphor and reality and we can see them as products of the soul's continuous morphing.

This essential morphogenic plasticity of our souls not only leads us forward on our personal mission on this planet, but also allows glimpses of the promise of freedom inherent in human nature. The soul can be characterized as the dominant part of the self that experiences, perceives, observes, acts, thinks, makes choices, responds, enjoys, suffers and remains the inner abode of all these elements. The whole Universe outside us dwells in our innerness—the macrocosm in the microcosm. Sufi mystics and poets have, over the centuries, written volumes on the *qatra* (droplet) containing within itself the dariya (river).

We deal with aeronautical problems in Euclidean geometry, wherein each dimension is a straight line that intersects other dimensions at right angles. In more complex problems, we use Riemannian geometries where dimensions do not intersect at right angles, as in the surface of a sphere. Inner experience sometimes appears Euclidean, at a simplistic cause and effect level, but most of the time it is Riemannian. Recently, I visited my birth place Rameswaram. I was standing on the shore watching the motion of the waves, something I used to do as a child. Each wave to me represented an individual. A new insight emerged as to how each wave is distinct from others, and yet is not independent of other waves, or of the ocean itself.[1]

My friend and co-author of *Wings of Fire*, Arun K. Tiwari, had a long series of dialogues with me during his several visits to Rashtrapati Bhavan and on our travels together. On many occasions we sat in the Immortal Hut in the Mughal Garden where he worked on his laptop as I fielded his questions and poured out my thoughts on topics of mutual interest, and if I may say so, of Universal value. He later appended to our conversations, relevant passages from various texts which I had highlighted in my readings and expanded the thought process into a free-flowing conversational text. In Indian culture, the relationship between the master and the pupil dictates that some of the pupil's attributes inevitably become an integral part of the teacher's qualities. Arun has accomplished the rare and difficult feat of making the teacher imbibe some of the pupil's qualities.

This book is organized into three parts. The first part deals with the concept of inner experience—thoughts, images, emotions, feelings, sensations, perceptions, insights and knowledge among other things. In the second part, the essence of some great souls is presented—people who lived in different eras and who could offer to mankind a movement forward in the most selfless manner. We have included, without any hesitation, some luminaries from contemporary times in this list of great people. It is relatively easy to look at greatness and judge it from a distance in time. But to see it in others around you is a little difficult, but at the same time, very important. In the third and concluding part, the book describes the journey of the soul and its various manifestations as the unfolding of an eternal essence.

The human race is called the last and the foremost by the Prophet of Islam (peace and blessings be upon him). This is so because, although man was the last creature to come into existence, he is, in fact, the focus and goal of creation. When our knowledge from the past structures our experience in the present, there is a danger of reality getting obscured. Time and again humanity has blindly and thoughtlessly repeated its past blunders condemning young generations to find their way afresh in the darkness of basic ignorance. It is this ignorance that this book attempts to dispel. The dialouge in the book is not conclusive. I invite readers to interact and keep exploring the purpose of human lives. Afterall, we are all *Musafirs* (travellers).

> The water in your jug
> Is brackish and low
> Smash the jug
> And come to the river.[2]

A.P.J. Abdul Kalam

Contents

Part I

PERPETUITY 1

Part II

GUIDEPOSTS 45

Part III

THE ESSENCE 109

Notes 149

Acknowledgements 157

Bibliography 159

Index 163

Part I

PERPETUITY

I climbed and climbed;
Where is the peak, my Lord?
I ploughed and ploughed,
Where is the knowledge treasure, my Lord?
I sailed and sailed,
Where is the island of peace, my Lord?
Almighty, bless my nation
with vision and sweat:
Resulting into happiness,
With perseverance that outlives perpetuity.

Arun K. Tiwari (A.T.): Sitting under this great Banyan Tree is such a profound experience. What a beautiful bamboo hut have the artisans from Tripura made!

A.P.J. Abdul Kalam (A.P.J.): I have named it *Immortal Hut*[3].

A.T.: Why this name?

A.P.J.: Sitting here, I can feel in me something that is immortal. I can see the world as an external dramatisation of an internal phenomenon.

A.T.: But Sir, the internal world is so chaotic, clouded with confusion. Indeed a kaleidoscope of feelings and emotions, constructing images, now this, now that. On the other hand, the world moves in a very systematic manner.

A.P.J.: The Universe moves in a systematic manner. The world does not. But then, as there are laws governing the external world, like the law of gravity, the laws of aerodynamics, there are laws governing your inner world. You can understand your experiences better by observing these laws. Once you are in touch with your Self, you are activated as the hub of the Universe.

A.T.: To be the hub of the Universe is such a great feeling! But what exactly does it mean?

A.P.J.: As a hub of the Universe, you can see that there are no random acts. That we are all connected. That you can no more separate one life from another than you can separate a breeze from the wind.

A.T.: What a beautiful idea, an eternal interconnectedness. Things that happen before you are born still affect you. And people who come before your time affect you as well.

A.P.J.: The idea of eternal interconnectedness implies that all endings are also beginnings. We just don't know it at that time. We are all creatures with some profound meaning that we may not know.

A.T.: Like the afterlife of a butterfly is not known to the caterpillar.

A.P.J.: We cannot think more than that, we are all parts of some splendid design. This whole Cosmos is not just running on and running down, without meaning. Each of us can have the belief of acting in this grand drama.

A.T.: Well, Sir, everywhere around, there is so much hardship, suffering and pain. A very large number of people will not find this thought of living a grand drama palatable.

A.P.J.: Individual acceptance of reality is so insignificant. It is indeed meaningless—sheer vanity, a futile boast of a feeble mind. There are difficulties but there is also so much love, beauty and joy around us. When we make ourselves blind to the abundant beauty around us and keep on looking at our selfish problems, suffering is only natural. We have to be open to the life in the adventure of human personhood.

A.T.: Why don't we do that?

A.P.J.: Because we erroneously consider ourselves as the

centre of our life. We expect everything to happen our way and to our benefit.

A.T.: That is so very natural to expect. Isn't it?
A.P.J.: It is so very common, but not natural in any way. What does one bring to this life? Does not each one of us come into this world empty-handed, naked and crying?

A.T.: Yes, but we do bring with us a genetic pool.
A.P.J.: Who brings it? It comes naturally. That is our essence, the essence of a human being. But soon this essence is covered with a name, a web of relationships, expectations, responsibilities, ambitions and demands.

A.T.: Yes. That is how a human being becomes a person. A unique self emerges out of every child.
A.P.J.: What way unique? Only some stereotyped self. Or, perhaps *a presence disconnected from its essence*, would be a better phrase. It is this alienation of an individual self from the essence of human being that is the source of much suffering and hardship in life.

A.T.: How do I make contact with my essence? Draw from it?
A.P.J.: We can do that by bringing out our thoughts, feelings, words, and actions into alignment with our understanding of God's will.

A.T.: That shouldn't be a problem.
A.P.J.: The Holy Quran says: "We proposed faith unto the heavens, and the earth, and the mountains: and

they refused to undertake it, and were afraid of it; but the human being undertook it: and yet truly, he was unjust to himself, and foolish."[4]

A.T.: Very stern words. You have brought out a very interesting concept here—the alienation of self from the essence. To an average mind, both appear the same. I am a human being and my identity is myself.

A.P.J.: I believe my true being is my essence. My self is a label that I wear. Sometimes it is only reduced to a mask.

A.T.: Then, who is the real me?

A.P.J.: To me, the word 'soul' offers the best description of what a human being actually is. The self, the identity of presence, is a construct of the world—you are given a name, you live with certain relationships, hold a certain position in society, and so on.

A.T.: The self as a construct of the world. The Buddha called it *nama* and *rupa* (name and form).

A.P.J.: Sage Ashtavakra writes in *Ashtavakra Gita*[5]: "You are neither earth, water, fire, air nor even ether. Know yourself as consisting of consciousness, the witness of these five."[6]

A.T.: A mere witness? But then what is consciousness? Where does it dwell?

A.P.J.: Consciousness is not a construct. It is eternal. It continues. It is indeed a continuum. It is beyond mind, which is of course beyond the brain.

A.T.: The Bhagvad Gita says: "Soul is invisible, inconceivable and immutable. It is ever-lasting, it dwells in all things. Weapons do not cleave it, fire does not burn it, water does not wet it, and wind does not dry it. It always is."[7]

A.P.J.: Yes, indeed. The concept of a divine continuity through human generations is included in all major religions of the world.

A.T.: Will you please elaborate on it?

A.P.J.: There are traditional concepts designating various psycho-spiritual organs or, sometimes, faculties of sensory and supra-sensory perception. In the Holy Quran, psyche finds mention as *nafs*.

A.T.: Is *nafs* an Arabic word?

A.P.J.: Yes. Understood in contemporary language, *nafs* is a term for the baser, lower, egotistical and passionate facets of human nature which, along with *tab* (literally, physical nature), comprises the vegetative and animal aspects of human life. Some of the other synonyms for *nafs* are devil, passion, greed, avarice, ego-centredness, etc.

A.T.: So *nafs* is not soul.

A.P.J.: No. The soul is *ruh*. The central aim of a good human life is the transformation of *nafs* from its deplorable state of ego-centredness through various psycho-spiritual stages to a state of purity and submission, to the will of God.

A.T.: What are these various psycho-spiritual stages?

A.P.J.: The Holy Quran provides a very deep understanding of the psycho-spiritual phenomena that go through a human life. A clear distinction is made between *nafs, qalb, sirr* and *ruh*.

A.T.: Please explain.

A.P.J.: The term *qalb* stands for the heart which is the cradle of thoughts and emotions. This heart is the seat of beatific vision, as well. But, for the vast majority, it is the battleground of two warring armies: those of *nafs* or passion, and *ruh* or spirit. Cleaning of the *qalb* is a necessary element in spiritual discipline for travellers on the right path.

A.T.: And what is *sirr*?

A.P.J.: The faculty of *sirr* is believed to be located in the middle of the chest, where the physiological heart exists. By emptying of the *sirr* we mean diverting one's attention from the mundane aspects of human life and fixing it on the spiritual realm.

A.T.: You have used two different verbs—cleansing of *qalb*, and emptying of *sirr*.

A.P.J.: I am happy you are getting into the concept. The emptying signifies negation and obliteration of ego-centred human propensities. *Ruh* is a dormant spiritual faculty that needs to be worked upon by constant vigil and prayer, in order to achieve the illumination of the spirit.

A.T.: It appears so systematic and orderly.

A.P.J.: There is a well-defined sequence of actions. The

purification of elementary passionate nature (*tazkiya-e-nafs*), followed by cleansing of the spiritual heart so that it may acquire a mirror-like purity of reflection (*tazkiya-e-qalb*), fortified by emptying of egoic drives (*taqliyya-e-sirr*) and remembrance of God's attributes (*zikr*), gloriously culminating in illumination of the spirit (*tajjali-e-ruh*) – this is the essential spiritual journey.

A.T.: There seems to be a lot of inner work involved.

A.P.J.: Yes. Life is a torturous inner journey involving great hardships.

A.T.: Subhash Kak[8] in *Prajna Sutra* (Aphorisms of Intuition) terms life as "a flight across desert or unending waters...it will not be fun."

A.P.J.: Flying is a good metaphor. *Prajna Sutra* is published recently?

A.T.: Only last year, Sir. It is indeed contemporary wisdom. Subash Kak sees the unfolding of self as a flight. The essence is in motion. That is the primary experience. Gulzar said the same thing in *Parwaaz*[9].

A.P.J.: Experience is a cyclical phenomenon. A spiral structure would be a better simile. Each time you return to the same point, you would have expanded.

A.T.: What is the purpose of this expansion?

A.P.J.: Many mystics called this world a theatre of myriad themes and characters. The purpose of life can be seen as to provide certain lessons for which the soul is an observer. The soul is expected to discern the various subtle dimensions of reality and enriches itself by integrating to this ground.

A.T.: Can we call this a process of transformation?

A.P.J.: Unfolding would be a better word. Through the unfolding of the soul, a human being becomes not only a microcosm and mirror of reality, but also its agent, organ and servant. After all, reality also needs to be worked upon. That is the original deal.

A.T.: Man as the "agent, organ and servant of God Almighty"[10] is a sacred thought.

A.P.J.: You may call it the expression of an inner transformation of consciousness that I might have undergone.

A.T.: I've always admired your self-effacing humility.

A.P.J.: What else is there? Is there anything we can boast of? As an individual, you are asking some questions that I am trying to answer. How can you say that the content of our conversation is a product of our collective intellect? The real source of this content can also be seen as manifestation of the essence of our souls and what we ultimately are.

A.T.: Yes, that's possible. One needs to be enlightened enough to understand it this way.

A.P.J.: One needs to thrust aside the reasoning mind in order to become enlightened. Smash the jug and come to the river.

A.T.: You mean one should have a spiritual outlook

rather than be preoccupied with worldly concerns and worries?

A.P.J.: Both are important. I believe that integration between the worldly and the spiritual can be achieved harmoniously.

A.T.: At least at the beginning, we have only ourselves as the agents of knowing, the organs of perception, and the locus of the revelation of truth. What is the 'I' that we want to know and understand?

A.P.J.: Our true or spiritual nature does not need any kind of modification or alteration. It is primordially pure and complete. However, we need to work on ourselves, *tazkiya-e-nafs*, in order to become sufficiently open and clear to even have a glimpse of this nature, *tajjali-e-ruh*.

A.T.: To be open to our soul, you mean?

A.P.J.: Exactly. And it is not optional. It is very necessary. It is indeed mandatory. The great Sufi poet Moulana Jalaluddin Rumi writes:

> Hungry, you're a dog, angry and bad-natured.
> Having eaten your fill, you become a carcass;
> You lie down like a wall, senseless.
>
> At one time a dog, at another time a carcass,
> How will you run with lions, or follow the saints?[11]

A.T.: So, life entails a lot of responsibility.

A.P.J.: A matter of real hard work and discipline.

A.T.: I have shown you hundreds of letters that readers of *Wings of Fire* have written, saying that reading the book had transformed their lives. It was indeed such a great and satisfying feeling. How do we understand this phenomenon? Something in *Wings of Fire* triggered something that was already present within the reader.

A.P.J.: Thoughts do not come from outside; neither do feelings or images. They come from the soul and go back to the soul, always within the soul. Somewhere, there was an expression of my essence in *Wings of Fire* and this essence found resonance with the essence of many readers. We spoke about the oneness of humanity—what Islamic thinkers have aptly termed *Wahadat-e-Insaniyat*[12]. At the core of it, we're all connected.

A.T.: Can we say that essence, the soul, is one's real self?

A.P.J.: You need to look beyond definitions. Don't try to define the word 'soul'. Attempt to understand the phenomenon of life. As I understand it, the soul is the locus, the agent, and all the varied content of human experience.

A.T.: But who undergoes these experiences?

A.P.J.: We fool ourselves by seeing the mind as something residing in our body. We normally look at ourselves, including our consciousness, through the filter of our perception and worldview. The reality is just the opposite. The mind is an ocean; it contains so many worlds within itself, mysterious, dimly seen.

A.T.: And our body is a cup, floating on the ocean; soon it will fill, and sink.

A.P.J.: Excellent! This is what happens most of the times, with most people. When we can experience ourselves without this filter we experience ourselves directly, immediately, and intimately. Keep floating, receiving the sunlight, the moonlight and the breeze.

A.T.: The crux, therefore, is not to be prisoners of our minds.

A.P.J.: More than that, to live a purposeful life. What if you are a jar full of water and yet the rim is always dry?

A.T.: How do we do that?

A.P.J.: Man is the only creature engaged in the pursuit and advancement of knowledge on this planet, perhaps in the known Universe. Knowing is the fundamental characteristic of every moment of our experience. Our sensation is knowledge of sensation; our emotion is knowledge of emotion. Our seeing is knowledge, our hearing is knowledge, our thinking about the past, present and future is knowledge. Our questioning is knowledge. Our sense that we don't know something is knowledge.

A.T.: Will you please give an example?

A.P.J.: At a pedestrian level of thought, you know that someone has been disrespectful to you. On a higher plane of awareness and understanding, you know that you feel hurt and angry. You know the sensation of the physical tensions and impulses which are a part of your reaction. You know the words you want to say to your friend.

A.T.: How do we do that?
A.P.J.: To inhibit our inner field completely, in all its richness and freedom.

A.T.: What will happen then?
A.P.J.: Ignorance will get dispelled.

A.T.: In fact we know many things that aren't true.
A.P.J.: This wrong knowledge is generated out of our wrong beliefs and even inaccurate perceptions. Every impression involves knowing. Every experience is knowledge. Knowledge is the very fabric of experience.

A.T.: Human essence, then, is not simply an organism of consciousness, but is also an organism of knowledge.
A.P.J.: You are right. Traditional teachings of spiritualism and philosophy describe the process of realisation, as waking up to reality. An oft-used analogy is that of an individual mistaking a rope for a snake when his vision is veiled and obscured by ordinary experience and then, waking up to the fact that it is indeed a rope.

A.T.: Does it mean that knowledge contains all experiences, including illusion?
A.P.J.: Sage Ashtavakra says: "Just as a mirror exists as part and apart from its reflected images, so the

Supreme Lord exists as part and apart from this body."[13]

A.T.: Some things in our experience constitute information, other things are issues, yet others are feelings, and some things are objects, and so on. How do we proceed deeper? How do we discern?

A.P.J.: If we perceive them on a mundane plane of thought and experience, directed by the ego, this is how things would appear. As we become aware of the ground that connects various elements, apparently separate from each other, the connecting ground emerges as the presence, consciousness, and basic knowledge.

A.T.: Ramana Maharshi[14] described it very nicely. "True nature is that of infinite spirit. When the mind unceasingly investigates its own nature, it transpires that there is such a thing as mind. This is the direct path for all."

A.P.J.: One of the most difficult things for a powerful mind is to be its own master.

A.T.: Do you think this is possible?

A.P.J.: Our thoughts are, most assuredly, things. They are conceived in the mind and travel through time and space like ripples in a pond affecting all that they touch. Thoughts are the building blocks of our experience. The world we see is the one we have created with our thoughts. Since time immemorial, philosophers and thinkers have looked into various dimensions of reality. Of course, modern genetics and physics are looking into the origin and the destination of what is seen at the present moment.

A.T.: There are controversies and debates, though.

A.P.J.: Controversies and debates are the preoccupations of lesser minds. Basic knowledge is uninfluenced by opinions or projections, and is not determined by prior constructions. The important point is that when we explore the forms of basic knowledge, it reveals to us its truths, its unvarying patterns and Universal principles.

A.T.: How do we define truth?

A.P.J.: The best I can tell you is what the German philosopher Friedrich Nietzsche[15] said: "Truth is the discipline of the ascetic, the quest of the mystic, the faith of the simple, the ransom of the weak, the standard of the righteous, the doctrine of the meek, the challenge of the mature."

A.T.: You mentioned this thought on 15 October, 2003 with Acharya Mahaprajna[16] at Surat. Fifteen spiritual leaders signed a Spiritual Declaration on that day.

A.P.J.: It was a great event. I felt blessed, with so many Spiritual Masters around.

A.T.: Incidentally, it was your 72nd birthday.

A.P.J.: I had completed 72 orbits around the Sun.

A.T.: You are very modest.

A.P.J.: What else is there? God took millions of years to create man. However He integrated in man the innocence and purity of the angelic spirit, and the deceit and bestiality of Satan. He, then, commanded His creation to use all faculties with reasoning to reach His image. This is the mission of human life.

What else is a human life but a name and form
Driven by hunger, tattered in reason:
Part god, part angel, part beast...
Rarely releasing its cryptic charm.

A.T.: The faculty of reasoning has interesting facets to it. In *The Inner Journey Home* A. Hameed Ali[17] (*pen-name*—AH Almaas) writes about an interesting 'thought experiment.' May I narrate it?

A.P.J.: Go ahead.

A.T.: Let us imagine that we are in a completely dark room, a room full of all kinds of objects. There is a light source in this room, with a dimmer switch that can be enhanced or reduced. We are also wearing clear eyeglasses with shutters of different colours. The coloured glass of each shutter has some transparent designs engraved on it.

A.P.J.: Then?

A.T.: We begin to increase the intensity of the light by sliding the dimmer slowly, to the dimmest illumination. We begin to see the vaguest outlines of some of the objects in the room. This is the beginning of basic knowledge.

A.P.J.: Seeing what is actually there.

A.T.: Yes Sir. But we see only dim outlines with and within shadows. We may misapprehend what we see, for we still cannot differentiate the shadows from the real objects. Our predicament is complicated further because of the multi-shuttered glasses.

A.P.J.: Our knowledge here, then, is incomplete because of the dim light and distorted by the colours and designs of the shutter glasses.

A.T.: But all of what we see is taken as knowledge. We turn the dimmer up slowly and steadily, and every once in a while, remove one of the shutters in our glasses. Basic knowledge increases steadily, becoming fuller and more accurate. Each time we remove one of the shutters, we are surprised by what we see, amazed at the folly underlying our assumptions or the accuracy of our intuitions. Our knowledge becomes both complete and objective, both full and truthful.

A.P.J.: It is indeed a very apt parallel. The situation of having only a little light with shuttered glasses is the situation of a conventional experience, what I was referring to as an ego-driven experience. There is a lot of 'I' through which we take in anything.

A.T.: Hameed Ali described the shutters as the various ego structures that constitute the sense of self, and the design on each shutter is the integration of the history that went into the development of the structure.

A.P.J.: What is the message?

A.T.: The book says that the room is our soul. To know

what it contains, the illuminations must increase; the shutters and the eyeglasses must be discarded.

A.P.J.: Fantastic!

A.T.: Can we develop further the concept of soul as a knowledge system?

A.P.J.: Most of us assume that we have a great deal of knowledge only to realize in the later years of our lives how meagre, and incomplete it was, and how it will always remain inadequate and meagre, in contrast to the infinite vastness of potential knowledge.

A.T.: You mean knowledge is infinite?

A.P.J.: How can knowledge be finite? When we open up to pure knowledge, we are then in touch with the knowledge potential in consciousness, the inexhaustible source of all possible knowledge. When we need to learn something specific about the soul, the mind, essence, or reality, we can simply turn our attention there and we will discover that we are guided.

A.T.: If I may use a metaphor, it is like visualising that I am a seed, rather than the tree. I experience life stirring vibrantly inside the seed and recognize that this has the potential to be a tree. I do not experience the tree; I do not yet know what it is like to be a tree, or any particular kind of plant.

A.P.J.: It is a good analogy. Experiencing our soul as potential, we recognize that we are, more than anything else, the potential for experience, and for whatever is possible in experience. The soul is at the root, pure potential, potential for consciousness, knowledge, experience, life, growth, learning, expansion, and so on. Rather, we are potential itself, pure potential.

A.T.: Life as a potential is a great thought.

A.P.J.: All of our life is nothing but the unfolding of this potential.

A.T.: How do we understand this potential? Is it a gift, a certain blessing?

A.P.J.: This is the normal meaning of potential, but this is only a part of our potential. Our potential is not just the sum total of the gifts, special qualities and abilities that we have. Our potential is everything we have ever experienced, everything we will ever experience, everything we can ever experience.

A.T.: It can't be therefore quantified?

A.P.J.: When Joshua, the successor of Prophet Moses (*Hazrat Musa Alaih Assalaam*) lay dying, he wept in sadness. When the Rabbi asked him why he was weeping, Joshua said that he was crying because he could not do what Prophet Moses (*Alaih Assalaam*) had achieved. The Rabbi said, "God will not ask you about what Prophet Moses (*Alaih Assalaam*) had done, He will ask you about what you had done?" The potential is given. The point is actualising the potential.

A.T.: How does this happen—potential becoming actuality?

A.P.J.: How does the seed become a tree—that seems to be your question?

A.T.: No Sir. My question is about the inner work in a human life.

A.P.J.: To explore this, we first need to remember that our essence is not a particular state or condition; nothing that has come as a packet or heirloom from somewhere. It is the medium and locus where all states and conditions arise. When you know the truth about who you really are, you may indeed be free.

A.T.: The Buddhist concept of *anatman*, No-Self, says just that.

A.P.J.: You are right. Let us understand it. When we analyse our experience, we notice that experience is in a state of constant and continuous change and transformation. One thought follows another, one feeling leaves only to create space for another. Inner sensations and movements are never still.

A.T.: Our inner space is like a multiple intersection at the centre of a major city, where all streets and lanes are busy most of the time, with an incessant flow of traffic of various kinds and sizes of vehicles.

A.P.J.: Good analogy. Our inner space is not only busy with content; it is in incessant movement, transformation, development, evolution or devolution, expansion or contraction, and so on.

A.T.: It appears to be a powerful dynamic situation.

A.P.J.: Yes, it is indeed very dynamic. An important

property of our essence is its changeability. It is a fluid medium that flows in our body as well as through life around.

A.T.: It must be a great feeling, a sort of bliss.

A.P.J.: When we experience directly the flow of our essence in our activity, we feel we are flowing, not hampered, hindered or stuck. Our energy is unified, our mind focused, everything moving in an integrated, fluid and smooth fashion. We are completely involved in whatever we are doing.

A.T.: How do we get into this flow?

A.P.J.: The flow is not a displacement of something to somewhere else; it is not something flowing out from something else, but an unfolding consciousness that is manifesting its potential by steadily opening up.

(Kalam picks up a rose in the Mughal Garden.)

We can experience our soul as a rose unfolding and opening up, revealing the implicit forms in her potential. Our soul is an unfolding living rose with an infinite number of petals, each petal an experience, a perception.

A.T.: It is indeed such a striking concept. The whole idea of 'I' as a potential unfolding to infinite possibilities is so positive!

A.P.J.: Instead of 'I', let us say life—life is a potentiality. Perhaps that is why it is said that God created Man in His own image. He operates through humanity by creating billions of different potentialities on this planet and let them unfold to His Will. All manners of trades like tailoring, building, harvesting, goldsmithery, astronomy, medicine—*ad infinitum*—have been discovered from within man, His skills and abilities.

A.T.: We can see so many people deeply stuck and lost in the web of their worldly constructs. Trades have become jobs, skills have become services, and business has become commerce and money in a world that is being engulfed by consumerism.

A.P.J.: The great metaphor of a spider[18] exactly explains that. Our perceptions of truth are vulnerable and easily distorted by the web of ignorance, spun by the spider of the mind.

A.T.: I have a Chinese friend, Ji Ping.

A.P.J.: I met him. He translated *Wings of Fire* into Chinese.

A.T.: Yes Sir. Ji Ping told me about a story.

Meng Tzu[19] was asked, "We are all human beings. Why some are great men and some are small men?"

Meng Tzu replied, "Those who attend to their greater selves become great men, and those who attend to their smaller selves become small men."

"But we are all human beings," the inquirer continued. "Why is that some people attend to their greater selves and some attend to their smaller selves?"

Meng Tzu replied, "When our sense of sight and hearing are distracted by the things outside, without the participation of thought, the material things act upon the material senses and lead them astray."

A.P.J.: Fantastic thought! The function of the mind is thinking: when you think, you keep your mind, and when you don't, you lose your mind. This is what heaven has given us.

A.T.: We have come back to the concept of *nafs*.
A.P.J.: You are right.

A.T.: Will you please elaborate on *nafs*?
A.P.J.: Well, *nafs* is full of ideas. To go beyond *nafs*, one must know how to unlearn, to perceive first that our minds are full of concepts, beliefs and ideologies, that one has made all kinds of assumptions from an early age.

A.T.: But that is what we all have—*nafs* enfolds large areas of what we see and know as culture.
A.P.J.: Cultures are like many-hued glasses. Just as these glasses make colourless light to assume colour for them, cultures colour human essence. Actually speaking, a person's acculturation is his bondage.

A.T.: Why should one want to get rid of this bondage? Why shatter the glass?
A.P.J.: Because these glasses are empty of any substance, different colours of the same light. They are unreal—trickery of the mediums. Take high and low. Where is high, where is low?

A.T.: But if that is so, where does one stand?
A.P.J.: Look at the Milky Way, our galaxy. It consists of about 200 billion stars, with our own Sun being

a fairly typical specimen. If a beam of light were to be shot around the Milky Way, it would take almost 250,000 years to complete its journey. Our solar system is in a spiral arm called the Orion Arm, and is about two-thirds of the way from the center of our galaxy to the edge of the starlight. The Earth is the third planet from the sun in our solar system of nine planets. In fact it is like a peppercorn on a 1000 yard walk.[20]

A.T.: If Earth itself is a peppercorn in the 1000-yard solar system, what is a human being?

A.P.J.: Be therefore humble. The Universe is not so destitute to need anyone's service. There is a power that created Universe. It will take care of it with or without a human's help. It is not that the Universe needs your service. You need to serve.

A.T.: But I, a human being, can think that which no other living creature in the known Universe can.

A.P.J.: And what do you think? Are not all our thoughts subjective? Examine your thoughts closely and you will see that they are either desires or fears. Then there is this polarisation of *me* and *not-me*. What else?

A.T.: That is true. But we do create, invent and develop new concepts.

A.P.J.: Only when the mind is still. Creation comes only when there is no anticipation. As long as you are looking forward to an experience, you are pursuing an achievement, the mind is in the saddle, the ego is in command, and nothing new can occur.

A.T.: You are giving a new insight. I have always aspired to be a thoughtful person.

A.P.J.: Thought has tremendous powers of projection, you can visualise all sorts of things, but it won't be real.

A.T.: Then what is one to do?

A.P.J.: Just be quiet and sit down. Mankind today is drunk—full of self-hatred, mocking other people's existence, robbing them of their riches, terror, bombing... and this is the edge of the roof.[21]

A.T.: But Sir, there are powerful explanations, arguments, justifications. Are we deluding ourselves in thinking that we have changed anything?

A.P.J.: I feel this is terribly important for all of us to see, that we are constantly deceiving ourselves when talking about a new man, a new idea, a new method. As long as we continue to approach everything from the standpoint of the old consciousness, we are merely rehashing, carrying on the same old way of life, giving fancy names to stale details.

A.T.: It is important then, to have fresh consciousness, a vision.

A.P.J.: Now you are getting to the point. Where there is no vision, the people perish.[22] Everyone needs dreams and a goal in order to live fully and satisfactorily.

A.T.: And from where would this vision come?
A.P.J.: From within, *tajjali-e-ruh*.

A.T.: And what do I do for that?
A.P.J.: To have mirror-like purity of observation, *tazkiya-e-qalb*, and freedom from distortions of perception, *taqliyya-e-sirr*.

A.T.: And what happens when the soul is illuminated?
A.P.J.: One who cultivates his higher self will find that his lower self follows in accord. The Gita gives you this assurance. Once you get to the higher plane you do not regress to the previous stage.[23]

A.T.: But why doesn't this generally happen?
A.P.J.: The polarisation of *me* and *not-me* does not allow that. Since we have highly subjective thoughts, we tend to have a proprietary claim on certain thoughts and cannot let go of them. We have vested interests, and that is the reason why we fail to achieve anything new, real. We condemn ourselves to the prison of our own making.

A.T.: It is shocking!
A.P.J.: I am happy that you are shocked. And remember, it happens at all levels—in families, communities, societies and between nations.

A.T.: And how does one stop this?
A.P.J.: It can't be stopped. It has to be faced and comprehended—and overcome.

A.T.: You mean difficulties.

A.P.J.: Look buddy, ordinary society, everyday life, is the best training school. From a spiritual point of view, the many shocks encountered in everyday life ought to be welcomed as a help in checking ourselves not to be cushioned or pampered.

A.T.: That is at the personal level. What happens at the level of society?

A.P.J.: Same thing. Globalisation is a shock to the indigenous industry. Stand up to it. Rise above it.

A.T.: Would it be possible?

A.P.J.: Why not? Competitiveness is the crown in the kingdom of sweat.

A.T.: *Kingdom of Sweat*! So we have the idea for our next book.

A.P.J.: Exactly. I always believed in the sacredness of sweat. The Universal power never judges or criticizes. It Only accepts us at our own value.

A.T.: We must get into the act.

A.P.J.: Make no mistake about it. If you want to know the taste of a fruit, you have to peel it, bite it, and chew it. Unless you follow the law of aerodynamics all you can have is a free fall.

A.T.: All genuine knowledge originates in direct experience.

A.P.J.: A seed germinates spontaneously but only when it is placed in tilled soil with moisture around.

A.T.: This is what the brain does with ideas—developing intelligence.

A.P.J.: The brain in itself is not intelligent. It is like a computer. You programme it and it will carry on its investigations, but at the end, the result of that search is always contained in the programme, in the mind. So it never discovers anything new. The best of brains are only supercomputers.

A.T.: But Sir, there are different types of persons, intelligent and dull.

A.P.J.: The notion that some persons are more gifted or qualified than others is erroneous. There is no merit where there is no trial. Till the experience stamps the mark of strength, cowards may pass for heroes. Experience stands between faith and falsehood.

A.T.: There is a widespread tendency to avoid direct experience and managing with concepts and hypotheses.

A.P.J.: Management by concepts and hypotheses without direct experience is an exercise in sloth and fantasy. When we executed the Integrated Guided Missile Development Programme (IGMDP), we had home-grown the entire management structure for two major projects.

A.T.: There is a trend to invite international experts and consultants.

A.P.J.: We must concentrate our mental energies. There are too many thoughts. Freedom from perplexity is required to undertake an activity greater than ourselves.

A.T.: Marcus Aurelius Antoninus[24] said, "The soul is dyed by thy thought."

A.P.J.: Good words. I can forgive a man of sloth but never a wicked one. If you are sleepy[25], you must sleep; but please sleep on the Way of God. And maybe some other seeker on the Way will awaken you from your fantasies and slumber.

A.T.: How do I immunize or insulate myself against wickedness? All external influences, even my own past experiences, prod me on to retribution and revenge.

A.P.J.: Revenge is foolish. You will be better off being an ordinary worldly human being capable of quiet observation and contemplation.

A.T.: But how can anyone do that? We see things; listen to words and experience events. Isn't that how the human mind operates?

A.P.J.: We must learn to discern. Dung and musk[26] seem the same to one whose nose is clogged. There are some stern words from Confucius: "He who offends against Heaven has none to whom he can pray."[27]

A.T.: But Sir, mind, as consciousness, has no form, no structure. My friends in the hospital clarified this point for me. It is indeed nothingness. The nothingness of a hard disc that contains everything you operate with, the nothingness of a vessel that holds the water, the nothingness of a book that is to be read.

A.P.J.: At some point, thought through identification becomes an entity; thought creates that entity—'you' and 'I'. And once this happens, that 'I' will continue to aggrandize it, build it up, and give itself security and sustenance as that entity.

A.T.: Can you give a concrete example?

A.P.J.: There are cats living in Rashtrapati Bhavan, and they pass from this side of the Mughal Garden to the other. But with all the beauty of the flowers and fountains around, all that they see would be nothing but the prey in a pigeon.

A.T.: It means the whole process is based on an inbuilt setting. One sees only the object of perception.

A.P.J.: Well, thought based on memory builds up consciousness as a solid entity, and then, a whole life is lived from that point of view, through that entity that has self-created boundaries and limits.

A.T.: You mean our perceptions are our own creation?

A.P.J.: The very mind that has created perceptions must go into itself and see how they have come into being; how the mind itself was born.

A.T.: How do we do that? How can I go into my own mind?

A.P.J.: You have to look at your motives, and see whether there is a psychological component in your relationships or not. You will surely discover how every action is driven by some psychosomatic entity.

A.T.: From where does our ultimate motive for action spring?

A.P.J.: Upon examination you will see that it always comes from the energy that keeps the psychosomatic entity intact, which is the energy of the ego.

A.T.: I will once again beg for an example. My intellectual leanings always make me look for metaphors.

A.P.J.: Metaphors are very important. In the story of Mahabharata the world is one huge battlefield and the real Kurukshetra is within you. The battle of the Mahabharata is still raging within. Ignorance is Dhritarashtra; the individual soul is Arjuna; the in-dweller of your heart is Krishna, the charioteer; the body is the chariot; the senses are the five horses; mind, egoism, mental impressions, senses, cravings, likes and dislikes, lust, jealousy, greed, pride and hypocrisy are your dire enemies.

A.T.: Sir, Jaya Row[28] in *Profile of the Perfect Person* mentions a powerful message from *Vivekacudamani*[29]. Five different species are mentioned that are destroyed by a weakness for one sense object. The examples she gives are a moth attracted by sight. It goes around the dancing flame and gets scorched to death. A deer lured by sound. Attracted by drumbeats it comes out of bushes and gets shot. A fish in its weakness for taste bites the bait. A bee is attracted by the smell. It enters the flower which closes in and destroys it. An elephant falls for touch. Restless in the mating season, it falls in the trap. Now, poor man has the appetite for all five.

A.P.J.: Manu Smriti[30] also highlights the power of the senses over human wisdom.

A.T.: I had a chance to browse through a translation by Bühler. The exact words used are *balavan indriyagramo vidvamsamapi karsati.*

A.P.J.: Great businesses are thriving on feasting for human senses.

A.T.: But what do we do?

A.P.J.: The first line of defence on your side is the senses. Next in line is the mind. The human being is the only species with an intellect with which he can control the senses. So fortify your intellect, reinforce it.

A.T.: How do we go about it? Is it a matter of personal endeavour?

A.P.J.: The effort has to be both at personal and social levels. There should be integrated action through a moral, ethical and spiritual foundation even in materialistic matters. The whole Universe is a supply chain.

A.T.: How should we implement this integrated action?

A.P.J.: We have to establish powerful linkages and trade offs between economic prosperity and religious enrichment. This is possible only through the unity of minds.

A.T.: You undertook a search for unity of minds.

A.P.J.: Yes. I had visited some great religious places in my country and abroad. You were with me in Tawang.

A.T.: Yes Sir. It was in October 2002. You visited Tawang, a *Shangri-La*[31] at an altitude of 3,000 meters in a misty corner of Arunachal Pradesh. In fact it was on your 71st birthday.

A.P.J.: The people there seem truly happy and tranquil, living under the kindly umbrella of one of the world's oldest Buddhist monasteries.

A.T.: You asked the Abbot about the secret of Tawang's tranquillity. Why could it not be everywhere?

A.P.J.: Yes. The chief monk told me that there was no 'I' and 'you' there. He said, "If you look at 3,000 years of our history, you'll find that this land has always stood for peace. It worked for peace and has lived for peace."

A.T.: Then you said that these days, peace does seem to be in short supply.

A.P.J.: The monk gave a very thoughtful reply. He said, "Paradoxically, the 'I' in you wants peace. But to get peace, you have to first get rid of the 'I' and 'me'."

A.T.: You wrote a poem that night.

"Remove I and me,
Ego go away.
Eliminate ego,
Hatred will vanish.
Hatred jettisoned,
Anger will disapper.
Free from Anger,
You will lead to violence-free mind.
Violence-free mind,
Will blossom into Peace."

A.P.J.: I had another rich experience in Bulgaria. In November 2003, I visited a tenth century monastery associated with the patron saint of Bulgaria, Ivan Rilski[32]. The monastery is set amidst mountains which were aflame with autumnal colours at that time of the year.

A.T.: This is the place which was destroyed by fire due to invasions at the beginning of the 19th century; the complex was rebuilt later and is now surrounded by a big fort.

A.P.J.: You are right. I went to the altar and sought the permission of the Reverend Bishop John to recite a part of the prayer of St. Francis of Assisi[33]:

> "Lord, make me an instrument of your peace;
> Where there is hatred let me sow love."

A.T.: I can see the point. The small part of life that one is looking at so intensely, so deeply, contains within itself the whole essence. There is something right now in the immediate here and now that you can work with, like an instrument in the hands of a master sculpture.

A.P.J.: Lifeless by itself and yet casting life into stone.

A.T.: A new meaning of human existence is emerging.

A.P.J.: Once you become an instrument, you become a part of what is going on at a much deeper level, inside the heart of the sculpture. It is this that I understand as 'beingness'.

A.T.: Robert Powell[34] says in *Dialogues on Reality* that one must strive to shorten the intervals whenever one is distracted from 'beingness'.

A.P.J.: Exactly. The more attentive you can be, the more aware you can be of your thought—with its deep-rooted habits, illusions and misunderstandings. The longer you can do that, the shorter will be the intervals of your inattentiveness.

A.T.: So, our consciousness is the only thing we can count on.

A.P.J.: Human consciousness is the primary reality. Whatever you perceive is not only in consciousness, it is also of consciousness. The whole world hangs by this very slender thread of consciousness. No consciousness, no world.

A.T.: I have experienced it, Sir. On 5 January, 2004, I had a cardiac arrest and later, I was resuscitated. For several minutes, I was without consciousness. For me, the world did not exist during that time.

A.P.J.: There must be a perceiver for the world to exist, always. They both represent one continuum. Suppose there was no sentience left at all, there would be no world. For whom would that world appear?

A.T.: I can now see that what I call my reality is no more than a dream.

A.P.J.: I am indeed delighted that you wake up to be with me at this moment.

A.T.: What if I conclude that I am nothing?

A.P.J.: That is not the point. It is what you call this 'I', that is nothing.

A.T.: What remains then?

A.P.J.: Unfolding of the infinite potential of humanity through a complex body-mind connection.

A.T.: And if that doesn't happen?

A.P.J.: Nature is never in a hurry. It operates in terms of millions of years. A human life of 80 or 100 years is nothing but a tiny fraction in Nature's work. A human life-time is just wasted if it is spent in an unawakened state or slumber.

A.T.: Am I right if I understand that more the potential that manifests, the wider and the deeper is our experience?

A.P.J.: You are right. Once this is realised, our sense of who we are expands. Also, what we can do gets enlarged. A seed not only germinates other seeds, or other kinds of seeds; it opens up and develops into a tree.

A.T.: When we think of our lives, we think in terms of content. Our life is our situation, engagements, relationships, activities, projects, interests, pursuits, social and work structures, and so on. We think of how we spend our time, what things we do, what we value and pursue, our expressions and creativity, and the physical and human spheres within which all these take place.

A.P.J.: Here lies the confusion. What you describe is not the content of life. It is actually the context in which our life takes place.

A.T.: Then what is life?

A.P.J.: Our life is what we experience of it. I will call it genetic continuum.

A.T.: What is genetic continuum?

A.P.J.: You see my name—A.P.J. Abdul Kalam. Here the letters A,P and J indicate my genetic line. Avul is my great grandfather. Pakir is my grandfather. Jainulabdeen is my father. I am a succession of a natural descent.

A.T.: What about inheritance?

A.P.J.: Every one of us has inherent desires, attraction and repulsion towards objects. You are born with some and during your life time you cultivate many more. The life of a very happy and healthy but poor person is any day better than the life of a very rich but sad or sick person. Of course, the poor have to be elevated. That is the mission of the State.

A.T.: Napoleon Hill[35] writes in *The Law of Success*: "The palace of a king becomes as a hovel of a peasant if harmony doesn't abound within its walls. The hut of a peasant may be made to yield more happiness than that of the mansion of the rich man, if harmony obtains in the former and not in the latter."

A.P.J.: Beautiful.

A.T.: Sir, how do we handle circumstances if external context does define us.

A.P.J.: Give your mind a higher mission, a nobler goal. The external context does not give us life; we give life to it. The Office of the President of India does not endow Kalam with life. When Kalam moves, they say the President of India is walking.

A.T.: Will you tell something more on this experience aspect?

A.P.J.: When we are in touch with ourselves, not in conflict with ourselves, not repressed or divided within, then we are more in touch with our essence, and this contact makes our potential manifest. This experience is inherent in life. A sense of inadequacy or the inability to come to terms with experience in its actual form, is tantamount to frittering away time or even life itself.

A.T.: How can I be a positive influence in the world?

A.P.J.: If you want to be a positive influence in the world[36], at first, get your life in order. Your behaviour influences others like a ripple travels through water. If your life works, you influence your family. If your family works, your family influences the community. If your community works, your community influences the nation. If your nation works, your nation influences the world. This is the true nature of human existence.

A.T.: What if these influences are bad?

A.P.J.: Life reflects back to us what we give it. Among the greatest gifts we may offer to our world are love, joy, peace, patience, kindness, goodness, faithfulness, gentleness and self-control. These are the gifts of a humble and sincere individual and come directly from the soul. The intellect by itself moves nothing. See all the good you can and bless the good you see.

A.T.: Buddhism has recognized the unique situation of the human being in positioning human life as the most auspicious of possibilities. In its teaching of transmigration, it postulates the idea that one can be born in various forms of life. It divides conscious beings into six categories[37]: gods, jealous gods, human beings, animals, ghosts and denizens of hell. Yet it believes that human life is far more precious than the others, even than that of gods, because it is the only form of the life where learning to the fullest extent is possible. Your last unreal you has come to your first real you to receive admonitions and gifts. But this real you is buried in another unreal you.

A.P.J.: I imagine one of the reasons people create unreal selves and cling to them so stubbornly is because they are scared to deal with their real selves. Willingness to risk failure and defeat is primary to growth.

A.T.: Sufi saint Hazrat Inayat Khan[38] says, "If you wish to know God, you must know yourself. How little man knows while he is in the intoxication of individualism?" Hazrat Inayat Khan sees the world as a dome, where every action is the echo of another.

A.P.J.: Introspection is essential. Make the most of yourself by fanning small sparks of possibility into flames of achievement.

A.T.: James Allen[39] writes in *As A Man Thinketh*, "You will become as small as your controlling desire; as great as your dominant aspiration."

A.P.J.: In man, good and bad are mixed. He is half angel and half beast. The real challenge lies in discerning.

A.T.: And how do we do that?

A.P.J.: What we would call virtues—courage, sobriety, innocence, serenity, humility, truthfulness, equanimity and detachment—are the tools to discern.

A.T.: Once you discern, how do you acquire the essence?

A.P.J.: You always have it. Each one of us has the *essence*, with all its aspects and dimensions, as part of the potential of our humanity. The problem is we do not seek it. This failure to realise inherent potential is the tragedy of the human condition.

A.T.: Is it possible that one can embody the essence, all the perfections of ultimate truth?

A.P.J.: It has always been possible. Human history is full of instances where the essence has been manifested through human lives.

A.T.: I think it would be worthwhile to discuss some such lives.

A.P.J.: Let me show you *Living with a Purpose* by S. Radhakrishnan.[40]

(Kalam goes to his study and reads from the book.)

"The truly great are not the men of wealth, of possessions, not men who gain name and fame, but those who testify to the truth in them and refuse to compromise whatever be the cost. They are determined to do what they consider to be right. We may punish their bodies, refuse them comforts, but we cannot buy their souls, we cannot break their spirits. Whoever possesses this invulnerability of spirit even to a little extent deserves our admiration."

A.T.: *Invulnerability of spirit* is the operative phrase here.

A.P.J.: You are right. The normal condition of human beings is a mix of virtues, and all the wretched and miserable characteristics in which humanity seems to specialize.

A.T.: What are the signs of a vulnerable soul? Carl Jung[41] says in *Man and His Symbols* that "the unconscious is no mere depository of the past, but is also full of germs of future psychic situations and ideas."

A.P.J.: When we experience the animal potential of the soul, we are then full of desires, cravings, uncontrollable impulses, lust and passion for what the world offers. We desire instant gratification, but our appetite for such gratification has no bottom and no end. We crave for more and more and more.

A.T.: How do we get rid of the bestiality of our soul?

A.P.J.: How can you get rid of it? The soul is indivisible. The great traditions of wisdom have recognized that a human being is mature and complete—that is, fully human—when the soul's essential nature gets fully integrated and harmonised with its animal potential.

A.T.: You mean the fully evolved human being retains animal instincts but integrates them into a perspective of selflessness and compassion.

A.P.J.: Jalaluddin Rumi has described the whole thing so beautifully:

> "Fiery lust is not diminished by indulging it,
> But inevitably by leaving it ungratified.
> As long as you are laying logs on the fire,
> The fire will burn.
> When you withhold the wood, the fire dies,
> And God carries the water."[42]

A.T.: People are distracted by objects of desires, indulging with phantoms. It drifts them farther from reality than before.

A.P.J.: When you dodge reality, you indeed tear off the wings which were given to bear you to Paradise. You go from this world lame, abandoned by a fantasy.

A.T.: Sir, this is thinking of life in its broadest sense—a matter of right choices.

A.P.J.: You are right. Life presents us with objects of desire to awaken our power of choice. Our essence is the invisible strength within us; when it recognises two opposite objects of desire, it grows stronger.

A.T.: You are talking like Pythagoras.[43] He said, "No man is free who cannot command himself."

A.P.J.: May be I am echoing Pythagoras. You are right. Commanding one's mind is fundamental. Freedom comes when the flickering flame of rambling thinking in the mind is made into a coherent laser of thought. In his great mind, Pythagoras formed one big picture envisaging mystic connections between numbers, spirits, souls, gods. Pythagoras indeed introduced the idea of eternal recurrence into Greek thought.

A.T.: Pythagoras argued that there are three kinds of men. The lowest are those who come to buy and sell, and next above them are those who come to compete. Best of all are those who simply come to look on.

A.P.J.: Man indeed blows into the bag of identities—selfhood, caste, religion, region, state, so many fabrications and impositions of this world—and fills it up. Then, one prick of the needle and he is emptied of air. How can intelligent people be so full of wind?

A.T.: You are right, Sir. We spread our intelligence over a hundred *important* affairs, over thousands of desires and concerns, great and small.

A.P.J.: You must unite the scattered parts. Redress wrong, aid all and injure none. Once you do that, deed by deed, from out of perplexity, then perhaps life will get a meaning that would outlive it. Unless you crush the wheat in a mill[44], how will there be bread on your table? Let us go back to our dream—the five people. Does not each one there remain alive in some way in this world?

□

Part II

GUIDEPOSTS

Master of the house I am not
Gardener maybe I.
Buds of prosperity blooming I care for
Safeguard fruits of compassion ripe.
Dream to see my country developed
Free from poverty, liberated from strife.

A.T.: Space, time and self are the three principal dimensions relating us to this finite world, through which each of us individually impinges on what we call reality.

A.P.J.: You are right about time and space but there is a problem with the self. The self is really nothing more than the conscious, localised, finite viewpoint of an individual in its surrounding society. A man to the society is what a cell is to the body.

A.T.: But isn't the cell that controls the body?

A.P.J.: No matter how vital this self-cell feels about it, its actual importance to society and the world is temporary and only educative.

A.T.: It is hard to comprehend how the self is effaced for the larger benefit of society; how one rises above the self for the greater good of humanity.

A.P.J.: Let me tell you about some people who could rise above their narrow perception of selves for the larger benefit of society. I will start with Emperor Asoka.

A.T.: You mean the third monarch of the Mauryan dynasty?[45]

A.P.J.: Yes. Asoka has come to be regarded as one of the most exemplary rulers in world history. The legend of Asoka is the story of a cruel and ruthless king who turned to *Ahimsa Dharma* and thereafter established a reign of virtue.

A.T.: Your example is very apt. Our nation has found

its emblem in one of a large number of edicts discovered in the Indian subcontinent. These edicts inscribed on rocks and pillars, proclaim Asoka's reforms and policies and promulgate his advice to his subjects. The rendering of these edicts offers us insights into a powerful and capable ruler's attempt to establish an empire on the foundation of righteousness, a reign which makes the moral and spiritual welfare of his subjects its primary concern.

A.P.J.: Asoka ascended to the throne after the death of his father, Bindusara. There seems to have been a two-year war of succession during which at least one of Asoka's brothers was killed. In 262 BC, eight years after his coronation, Asoka's armies attacked and conquered Kalinga, a country that roughly corresponds to the modern state of Orissa. The loss of life caused by battle, reprisals, deportations and the turmoil that always exists in the aftermath of war so horrified Asoka that it brought about a complete change in his personality. After the war, Asoka dedicated the rest of his life trying to apply Buddhist principles to the administration of his vast empire. He had a crucial part to play in helping Buddhism spread, both throughout India, and abroad. Asoka's reign lasted thirty-eight years.

A.T.: Asoka's edicts are mainly concerned with the reforms he instituted and the moral principles he recommended in his attempt to create a just and humane society.

A.P.J.: In his edicts, Asoka spoke of what might be called state morality and private or individual morality. The first was what he based his administration upon and what he hoped would lead to a more just and more spiritually inclined society, while the second was what he recommended and encouraged individuals to practice.

A.T.: Will you elaborate on the aspect of individual morality?

A.P.J.: The individual morality that Asoka fostered included respect towards parents, elders, teachers, friends, servants, ascetics and scholars. He encouraged generosity. The qualities of the heart that are recommended by Asoka in the edicts mirror his deep spirituality. They include kindness, self-examination, truthfulness, gratitude, purity of heart, enthusiasm, strong loyalty, self-control and love of the *Dharma*.

A.T.: We have no way of knowing how effective Asoka's reforms were or how long they lasted but Emperor Asoka has to be credited with the first attempt to develop a just and spiritual polity. Today, with widespread disillusionment in prevailing ideologies and the search for a political philosophy that goes beyond greed (market driven imperialism), hatred (ideological fundamentalism) and delusion (state is governed by the perfect), Asoka's edicts may make a meaningful contribution to the development of a more spiritually based political system.

A.P.J.: You are right. Another great man that stands as a guidepost to humanity is saint-poet Thiruvalluvar. He earned a living by weaving cloth and led an austere life. Thiruvalluvar was a man of few words—a man who could pack a wealth of meaning into two phrases.

A.T.: You are talking about the creator of *Kural*.

A.P.J.: Yes. Thiruvalluvar's *Kural* is regarded as a renowned work, eulogized as a directory of a code of conduct and ethics for humanity. It is called *poyyamozhi* or the 'book that never lies'.

A.T.: Tell me more about *Kural*.

A.P.J.: Written more than 2,000 years ago, the *Kural* enshrines in it 1330 couplets under 133 chapters. Each chapter comprising 10 couplets. The chapters fall under three major parts: Virtue, Wealth and Love. The first part known as *Arathuppal* (on Virtue), describes the greatness of an individual man. The second part, *Portutpal* (on Wealth), is the largest one with 70 chapters (700 couplets) covering the essentials of life in society. The third and last part, *Kamathuppal* or *Inbathuppal* (on Love), portrays the victory of inner self.

A.T.: As President of India, what teaching of Thiruvalluvar appeals to you the most?

A.P.J.: In the Tamil tradition, the head of the state is considered as the life and soul of society. He never fails in the following four qualities: fearlessness, liberty, wisdom and energy. He is a man of modesty and virtues and refrains from all vices; he is free from pride, anger and lust; he does not praise himself; he should be a man of self-control; he acquires wealth, guards it and distributes it to people; he is accessible and kind to all; he cares for his people, protects all who come to him; his friends are men of virtues and knowledge; he considers his ministers as his own eyes but examines their character and qualification before appointing them; he shows respect even to his enemies.

A.T.: What did Thiruvalluvar say about good governance?

A.P.J.: All the *Kurals* are primarily addressed to the king, but the Universal message they contain cuts across classes, and holds good for all. In modern times, democracies have replaced kingdoms and political parties and ministers have replaced kings. The qualities Thiruvalluvar attributes to kings are naturally expected to be found in our leaders: ministers, legislators, diplomats, planners, policy-makers, public office-holders and so on.

kaimmāru veṇṭā kaṭappāṭu mārimāṭṭu
eṇ ārruṅ kollō ulaku.[46]

Duty demands nothing in turn;
How can the world recompense rain?

A.T.: Is *Kural* relevant today?

A.P.J.: Perhaps more than ever before. In today's world of global competition, for success in any mission, we would essentially need indomitable spirit.

A.T.: What are the characteristics of indomitable spirit?

A.P.J.: It has two components. The first component is that there must be a Vision leading to higher goals of achievement. Take this *Kural*:

veḷḷat taṉaiya malarnīṭṭam māntartam
uḷḷat taṉaiyatu uyarvu.[47]

With rising flood the rising lotus flower its stem unwinds;
The dignity of men is measured by their minds.

If there is a solemn aim in one's life, irrespective of the hindrances and obstructions, the glow of the goal and our perseverance will nurture our souls, all through the surrounding difficulties, leading to success.

A.T.: What is your personal experience? You have gone through large programmes and projects. You would have experienced times when success is not in sight and there are many hurdles.

A.P.J.: I always kept Thiruvalluvar's wisdom close to my heart particularly in difficult times of my life. There is a *Kural*:

iṭumpaikky iṭumpai paṭuppar iṭumpaikku
iṭumpai paṭāa tavar.[48]

Grief they face and put to grief
Who grieve not grief by mind's relief.

It means successful leaders can never be defeated by problems. They become masters of the situation and defeat the problems.

A.T.: "Think and practice indomitable spirit to succeed" is the message.

A.P.J.: You are right. There is another *Kural*:

ul̤l̤uva tellām uyarvul̤l̤al maṟṟatu
tal̤l̤iṉun tal̤l̤āmai nīrttu.[49]

Let thoughts be always great and grand
Though they fail their virtues will stand.

We should never be defeated by any problem. We should become masters of the situation and defeat the problems bravely. I think these two *Kurals* characterize the indomitable spirit.

A.T.: I recently met Nobel Laureate Sir V.S. Naipaul[50]. He felt that our literature is largely power-centric. It focuses mostly on the affairs of the rich and powerful, and the concerns of the poor are not discussed.

A.P.J.: *Kural*, though addressed to those who are in charge of affairs of the state, does carry message for everyone. I also had a good talk with Sir Naipaul. He came with his wife. I found in him that uncanny ability of seeing the ways of the world. He has a perspective that comes of seeing events over a larger canvas of time—years, decades and perhaps centuries. He is very direct in his observation and perhaps brutally honest in his style and manner of narration. Both these traits are so central to *Kural*.

A.T.: What is the most powerful message *Kural* gives?

A.P.J.: The evils of poverty are personified in *Kural* as a sinner and a demon. When the demon takes possession of a person, the latter loses all joy in life. Poverty is cruel and it afflicts people; one may sleep in the midst of fire, but by no means in the midst of poverty and it destroys the greatness of the kingdom; poverty brings many miseries to a country. The words of the poor are profitless; the destitute that are too lazy to work consume their neighbour's salt and water; a poor man is a stranger to others; prolonged poverty destroys one's past greatness and the dignity of his speech.

A.T.: Where do we place *Kural*—amongst scriptures, perhaps?

A.P.J.: The *Kural* is neither a scripture nor an epic, but an extraordinary treatise on the art of living, which dwells deep into the unchanging and timeless foundations of human life and provides us with guidelines. Thiruvalluvar has examined all aspects of life and analysed life in its details and complexities.

A.T.: What fascinates you most in Thiruvalluvar?

A.P.J.: My fascination and respect for the saint-poet Thiruvalluvar is based on this: I have not come across any epic, or philosophy, or great works that are beyond the author's native land. In his 1330 Kurals, nowhere does Thiruvalluvar refer to any country or state he belongs to, or language, or religion. This Universal intellectuality of Thiruvalluvar overpowers me.

A.T.: What a great sweep of profound wisdom! India has really produced some great thinkers and philosophers.

A.P.J.: Not only thinkers and philosophers, but also scientists and rationalists.

A.T.: Whom would you call the foremost amongst the Indian scientists?

A.P.J.: Aryabhata. But why do we say Aryabhata is the foremost Indian scientist? Aryabhata gave the world the digit 'zero' for which he became immortal.

A.T.: I was not aware of this.

A.P.J.: We are never taught our own heritage in a proper way—there are only glorious myths and black holes.

A.T.: I came to know about Aryabhata only when India's first satellite[51] was named after him, and I was twenty then. The formal education I received was silent on Aryabhata's contribution to science.

A.P.J.: His book, the *Aryabhatiya*, presented astronomical and mathematical theories in which the Earth was taken to be spinning on its axis and the periods of the planets were given with respect to the Sun. Pythagoras also observed this fact though in more of a philosophical manner. The Greek later termed it as heliocentrism. It is interesting to know that as recently as in 1633, Galileo[52] was forced to recant his heliocentric views.

A.T.: Tell me more about *Aryabhatiya*.

A.P.J.: *Aryabhatiya* is written in 118 verses. Its mathematical section contains 33 verses giving 66 mathematical rules without any proof. There is a section of 25 verses on the reckoning of time and planetary models, and another section of 50 verses on the sphere and eclipses. The mathematical part covers arithmetic, algebra, plane trigonometry and spherical trigonometry. It also contains continued fractions, quadratic equations, sums of power series and a table of *sines.*

A.T.: Is it factual that Aryabhata discovered *pi*?

A.P.J.: What I know is that Aryabhata gave an accurate approximation for *pi.* He wrote in the *Aryabhatiya*, "Add four to one hundred, multiply by eight and then add sixty-two thousand; the result is approximately the circumference of a circle of diameter twenty thousand. By this rule the relation of the circumference to diameter is given." This gives value of *pi* as 3.1416 which is a surprisingly accurate value.

A.T.: India named its first satellite after Aryabhata.

A.P.J.: It was a fitting tribute. Aryabhata provided a systematic treatment of the position of the planets in space. He gave the circumference of the Earth as 4967 yojanas and its diameter as $1581^{1/24}$ yojanas. Since 1 *yojana* equals 5 miles, this gives the circumference as 24835 miles, which is an excellent approximation to the currently accepted value of 24902 miles. He believed that the apparent rotation of the heavens was due to the axial rotation of the Earth. This is quite a remarkable view of the nature of the solar system.

Aryabhata also gave the radius of the planetary orbits in terms of the radius of the Earth or Sun orbit as essentially their periods of rotation around the Sun. He believed that the Moon and planets shine by reflected sunlight; incredibly he believed that the orbits of the planets are ellipses. He correctly explained the causes of eclipses of the Sun and the Moon.

Aryabhata wrote that 1,582,237,500 rotations of the Earth equal 57,753,366 lunar orbits. This is extremely accurate and is perhaps the oldest astronomical constant known to man.

A.T.: How do you distinguish Aryabhata?

A.P.J.: Aryabhata is the first human to look at the Cosmos from the eyes of reason. I am in awe of his intellectual sweep—a profundity that returns nearly 1500 years later with Einstein.

A.T.: Let me take you to Islamic history. Who is your role model there?

A.P.J.: Role model would be a very big word for me to handle. But Caliph Umar ibn al-Khattab has been my most favourite. You read the dream sequence in *Ignited Minds*.

A.T.: What is the historical significance of Caliph Umar?

A.P.J.: The tender plant, which Prophet Muhammad (peace and blessings be upon him) left behind and the first Caliph Abu Bakr[53] had protected against storms, grew into a huge and sturdy tree that branched out in all four directions, under Umar's untiring care Islam became its human face as presented by the Prophet (peace and blessings be upon him).

A.T.: Where does the greatness of Umar rest?

A.P.J.: Umar's armies overthrew two mighty empires of the time. He took for Islam, Mesopotamia and parts of Persia from the Sassanids[54]; and Egypt, Palestine,

Syria, North Africa and Armenia from the Byzantines[55]. Rather than adopt the pomp and display affected by the rulers of that time, Umar continued to live, as he had lived when Muslims were poor and persecuted.

A.T.: He is remembered as the conqueror of Jerusalem.

A.P.J.: The legend is that the Greek Patriarch, Sophronius, inside the besieged Jerusalem, sent word out that he would surrender the city without a struggle, but only to Caliph Umar personally. Umar, then in Damascus, agreed and in one of the great scenes of Muslim history entered Jerusalem alone, except for a servant. Because his clothes were torn and dusty from the ride from Damascus, and because his manner to his servant was so courteous, the Byzantines, arrayed in pompous splendour to meet the victorious king, assumed the servant was Umar and greeted him effusively.

A.T.: Simplicity that underscores the greatness of power!

A.P.J.: Another legend has it that when the time of *Maghrib* (sunset) prayers came, Umar was in front of the church of the Holy Sepulchre. The Patriarch invited the Caliph to come inside and pray. Umar declined, saying that to do so might later encourage his followers to convert the church into a mosque. Instead he spread his headgear on the ground and prayed.

A.T.: Why are such events not remembered? Such acts are like beacon lights.

A.P.J.: A guidepost to humanity indeed. Umar made himself the fountainhead from which had flowed the undiluted blessings of the Holy Prophet Muhammad (peace and blessings be upon him) for mankind. Umar had learned to access his nucleus of calm. He handled the affairs of his life by not wasting his energy on maintaining peace between his conflicting fears and desires. He was able to face pain, sorrow and grief with equanimity. Nurtured by Caliph Umar, Islam should remain an ample field for the liberated mind and heart.

A.T.: Facing pain, sorrow and grief with equanimity is so central to your thought. I heard you mentioning that in the Golden Temple on 31 August, 2004.

A.P.J.: The Golden Temple, quite unfortunately, witnessed a lot of bloodshed. There was so much pain, sorrow and grief. However, peace prevailed, mainly because of the wisdom of the Gurus who provided light in the darkest hours of history.

A.T.: You composed a poem on your way to Amritsar. I remember a few lines from it:

"Four hundred orbits gone in no time
The great *Prakasham* has even out-glowed the Sun
As it orbits all around the Sun, even the Sun bows
in enhanced reverence
And salutes the Earth, for all that it carries
The greatest *Prakasham* of *Guru Granth Sahib*."

A.P.J.: You translated it into Hindi and recited at the

Golden Temple. See, I am drawn to men whose primary interest is not in any metaphysical doctrine but only in man and his fate.

A.T.: And that is what you see in Guru Nanak Dev.

A.P.J.: Yes. Guru Nanak Dev got enlightenment at the age of 27 when he started on his mission. After his enlightenment, his first statement was—"There is no Hindu, nor any Mussalman[56]." This is an announcement of supreme significance. It declared not only the brotherhood of man and the fatherhood of God, but also his clear and primary interest in man and his fate. There is an inalienable spiritual-moral combination in his message.

A.T.: Guru Nanak Dev toured extensively.

A.P.J.: Despite the hazards of travel in those times, Guru Nanak Dev performed five long tours[57] all over the subcontinent and to Arabia, as well. He visited most of the known religious places and centres of Hindu and Muslim worship. He explained and exposed through his preaching the incongruities, and fruitlessness of ritualistic and ascetic practices.

A.T.: Not only did Guru Nanak Dev proclaim equality of men in all respects, but in his system, the householder's life became the primary forum of religious activity. Life was not a burden but a privilege. Guru Nanak Dev made normal life as the medium of spiritual training and expression.

A.P.J.: Did you notice that throughout the later eighteen years of his mission, Guru Nanak Dev continued to work as a peasant. It was a total involvement in the moral and productive life of the community. To me, his life is a model to follow. By his personal example, he showed that leading a normal man's working life was fundamental to his spiritual system. In the Guru's system, idleness became a vice and engagement in productive and constructive work, a virtue.

A.T.: What is the most attractive thought of Guru Nanak Dev that you were drawn to?

A.P.J.: Guru Nanak Dev said, "Truth is high, higher still is truthful living."[58] His faith was simple and sublime. He lived by discipline—a way of life, a force, which connected one human being to another, as well as with the Guru.

A.T.: It is indeed the emphatic manifestation of his spiritual system into the moral formations and institutions that created a casteless society of people who mixed freely, worked and earned righteously, contributed some of their income to the common causes and the community kitchen.

A.P.J.: Guru Nanak Dev declared, "Without virtuous living there can be no devotional virtue."[59] Guru Nanak Dev expressed his doctrines through the medium of activities. He himself laid the firm foundations of institutions and trends which flowered and fructified later on. In that sense, he was the most powerful leader born on this land. Guru Granth Sahib contains the great thoughts of many religious leaders.

A.T.: Amongst the scientists of the modern era, who inspired you the most?

A.P.J.: In my view, Thomas Alva Edison was more responsible than anyone else for creating the modern world. Perhaps no one individual did more to shape the physical character of our present day civilization.

A.T.: Neil Baldwin[60] in *Edison: Inventing the Century* points out that little Edison, the last of seven children in his family, did not learn to talk until he was almost four years old. Another factor that very much shaped Edison's unique personality was his loss of hearing.

A.P.J.: You are right. In fact, Edison's disability-driven free-wheeling style of acquiring knowledge eventually led him to specifically question many of the prevailing theories on the workings of electricity.

A.T.: He is fondly remembered as a *lone eagle*.

A.P.J.: Well, he used his kaleidoscopic mind and his legendary memory, dexterity and patience to eagerly perform whatever experiments were necessary to come up with his own ideas and theories. In that sense, no doubt, he was a *lone eagle*.

A.T.: In *Edison: A Biography*, Matthew Josephson[61] writes that while most of Edison's contemporaries were indulging in popularized electrical dogmas of the day, he developed a style of dispassionately questioning them and boldly challenging them.

A.P.J.: Possessing a perspective always enables young

scientists to gradually establish a unique foothold in the world of practical science and inventions.

A.T.: Like you, Edison also dabbled with small-time business to earn his childhood expenses.

A.P.J.: Much more than me. All I did was distribute newspapers with my brother. At the tender age of fourteen, the precocious Edison had already started publishing his own little newspaper called *The Weekly Herald*, which was circulated on trains. This was indeed the first such publication ever to be typeset, printed and sold on a train anywhere. This mini-publishing venture netted him more than ten dollars per day even in those days. Most of it went towards setting up the chemical laboratory which he started in the basement of his home.

A.T.: How did opportunity knock on Edison's door?

A.P.J.: At the age of fifteen, Edison had pretty much mastered the basics of telegraph operators who had been called to serve in the Civil War. He used this opportunity to enhance not only his speed and efficiency in sending and receiving code, but also performing experiments designed to improve this device. His first authentic invention was an *automatic repeater*, which transmitted telegraph signals between unmanned stations, allowing virtually anyone to easily and accurately translate Morse code at their own speed and covenience.

A.T.: John H. Lienhard[62] tells in *the Engines of Our Ingenuity* that Edison made a beautifully constructed electric vote-recording machine. But when he tried to market it to members of the Massachusetts Legislature, they thoroughly denigrated it. A seasoned politician scolded him, adding that "Your invention would not only destroy the only hope the minority would have in influencing legislation, it would deliver them over – bound hand and foot – to the majority. This is exactly what we do not want."

A.P.J.: So politicians probably think in the same manner in all space and time.

A.T.: Edison learned from this, that one should never waste time inventing things that people would not want to buy. As if stung by rejection, he went on to create the most powerful medium of information. In 1903, he blended audio with silent moving images to produce *The Great Train Robbery*, and thus was born the Film Industry.

A.P.J.: That way, Edison led to the creation of so many things. When World War I[63] broke out, he was asked by the US Government to focus his genius upon creating defensive devices for submarines and ships. During this time, he also perfected a number of important inventions relating to the enhanced use of rubber, concrete and ethanol. All these inventions shaped the way mankind lived thereafter. When I read about Edison's work, I feel reverent.

A.T.: In the overall context of human affairs, who do you feel made the most difference to people's lives?

A.P.J.: Abraham Lincoln and Gandhiji.

A.T.: Lincoln was a part of the dream you narrated in *Ignited Minds*. He seems to be a part of your psyche.

A.P.J.: I don't know. Perhaps what Jung calls our collective consciousness would be a better idea. But working here in Rashtrapati Bhavan I draw so much from this great soul. His life was a great struggle, his task was so enormous. He presided over the Civil War. He faced so much criticism bravely.

A.T.: Facing criticism is indeed a very tough task. Once a leader is afraid of criticism he ceases to be a leader. He becomes a follower of the world around him—the officials, friends, media—eventually becoming a puppet in the show.

A.P.J.: Once Horace Greeley, founder editor of the influential *New York Tribune* had challenged Lincoln's failure to emancipate the slaves. He even questioned his lack of resolve on the issue in an editorial entitled *The Prayer of Twenty Millions*[64]. President Lincoln replied:

"I shall do less whenever I shall believe what I am doing hurts the cause, and I shall do more whenever I shall believe doing more will help the cause. I shall try to correct errors when shown to be errors, and I shall adopt new views so fast as they shall appear to be true views."[65]

A.T.: In that way, Gandhiji also faced the criticism of the world.

A.P.J.: That is how he became the Father of this Nation. Gandhiji did not buckle under criticism. He prevailed over it and in the process, shaped the way India lives today.

A.T.: You very often tell school children about Gandhiji, particularly his pain of seeing the events that marked our independence.

A.P.J.: You are right. When I woke up on 16 August, 1947, an adolescent that I was, I saw two pictures in the newspapers—Prime Minister Jawaharlal Nehru hoisting the tricolour flag of independent India on the Red Fort and Gandhiji fasting in Bengal. The pains of newly created nations were evident. Equally evident was the presence of a great soul—Mahatma—on the subcontinent.

A.T.: Gurudev Rabindranath Tagore had bestowed the *Mahatma* title upon Gandhiji shortly after his return from South Africa in 1915.

A.P.J.: Gandhiji and Rabindranath Tagore were great spiritual anchors to Indians in the midst of the storms of the freedom struggle.

A.T.: Rabindranath Tagore dreamt of a harmony of Universal humanity among the people of different origins through freedom of mind and spiritual sovereignty. He was the first-ever Asian writer to be awarded a Nobel Prize in 1913.[66]

A.P.J.: Rabindranath Tagore was the product of great Indian civilization, our voice as in a dream.

A.T.: With the title of *Mahatma*, the responsibility for India's problems became Gandhiji's own.

A.P.J.: Even before that people were more central to his thought. When I went to South Africa in September 2004, so many people told me that Gandhiji had radically changed the lives of Indians living in South Africa. Gandhiji taught them, "Non-violence is the greatest force at the disposal of mankind. It is mightier than the mightiest weapon of destruction devised by the ingenuity of man."[67]

A.T.: In *Gandhi: His Life and Message for the World*, Louis Fischer[68] writes that back in India, Gandhiji started a project (*ashram*) where people from different religions lived together in peace and freedom. He never made any secret of anything and was a nice and friendly person throughout his whole life. When he came back to India, crowds were already waiting and cheering him at the harbour and people celebrated his arrival. But that did not make him happy. He wanted to live like most of the people in India; out in the countryside and poor. He wanted to be one of them, one of the country he was born in but had been away from for so long. So he started travelling through the entire country by train in third class wagon. There he saw a thick cross-section of the real India and the manner in which most of his countrymen lived and worked. Very soon, he became the leader of the Indian Campaign for Home-Rule. The masses loved him because he was so close to them.

A.P.J.: It was only natural that he began to take the lead in the long struggle for independence from Britain. He asked the whole nation to strike for one day and they did. Nothing worked on that day. There was virtually no traffic, mail was not delivered, factories did not work and – for the British a very important thing – the telegraph lines did not work and they were cut off from their mother country. It was then that they first realized the reach and significance of Gandhiji's power in India.

A.T.: I was reading *Gandhi, The Man: The Story of His Transformation* by Eknath Easwaran[69]. In 1930, the spirit of the Dandi March illuminated India's way to independence. The British had control of the salt that was taken out of the sea. Indians had to pay tax for the salt. Gandhiji thought that control over the salt industry was one of the many hegemonic devices that constituted British rule in India. He started a march over 140 miles (about 200 kilometres) to the ocean. When he started, Gandhiji had only a few hundred followers but when they reached the sea they swelled to a mass of many thousands. People from many villages on the route decided to walk with them. When they arrived at the sea, Gandhiji took a handful of salt. That was a symbolic action and he asked everybody to do the same. After the police cleared them all away from the beach, they decided to walk into the salt factories and take salt from there. The British ordered the soldiers to stand before the gate to the factories and not let anyone in. The unarmed protesters walked to them and tried to walk in, only five at a time. And the soldiers hit them all until they could not walk any further. Women picked them up and took them away for nursing their wounds. No one on the side of the protesters used violence.

It was a very powerful display of the doctrine of non-violence. The civilized world shuddered.

A.P.J.: Most of Gandhiji's actions were a great success. The reason was that the British did not know how to act against an enemy (!) who did not use violence. But the important fact was that the media all over the world talked about Gandhiji and his actions because otherwise there would not have been enough public pressure upon the British officials. More and more people everywhere in the world agreed with Gandhiji when they saw the British violence against the non-violent people. And they loved him because he was so close to the people in his country. To work together with the Press and to have no secrets was one of the important features of his work.

A.T.: There is a lot of ambiguity on his views about religion.

A.P.J.: I see no problem. Nobel Laureate Octavo Paz[70] answered a similar question by saying, "Saints are not judged, they are venerated." When Muslim and Hindu compatriots committed acts of violence, whether against the British, or against each other, he fasted until the fighting ceased. Independence, when it came in 1947, was not a military victory. It was a triumph of human will. To Gandhiji's despair, however, the country was partitioned into India and Pakistan. The last months of his life were spent trying to end the appalling violence which ensued, leading him to fast to the brink of death, an act which finally quelled the riots.

A.T.: How do you reflect on Gandhiji's guidance?

A.P.J.: Gandhiji fought for the rights of those who were pushed down their whole life. He encouraged everyone to stand up for their rights and to fight against cruelty. He showed the whole world how easy it is to fight for one's rights and how successful this struggle can be, if people together fight for the same cause. Octavo Paz writes in *In Light of India*, "He (Gandhiji) wanted neither power nor glory; he sought to serve others, particularly the unfortunate. He proved it with his life and with his death."

A.T.: I can see that. Gandhiji set an example for struggling people wherever in the world.

A.P.J.: Some of the good examples are the struggle of the blacks in South Africa and in North America, as also that of the Amerindians in South America. Albert Einstein, among many others, praised Gandhiji's achievement; Martin Luther King Jr., the Dalai Lama and all the world's peace movements have followed in his footsteps. Gandhiji, who gave up cosmopolitanism to gain a country, has become, in his strange afterlife, a citizen of the world. I particularly remember Einstein's words about Gandhiji:

> "You have shown through your works, that it is possible to succeed without violence even with those who have not discarded the method of violence."[71]

A.T.: There are perceptions that Baba Sahib Ambedkar and Gandhiji differed on certain issues.

A.P.J.: Differed would be an inappropriate word. Both Gandhiji and Baba Sahib were men of the masses, true sons of this soil and leaders in the real sense of leadership. Gifted with power, virtue and excellence, both of them were New India personified. Polarity is fundamental in Reality. When the Sun arrives, sky is perceived as East and West. Where is the East? Where is the West?

A.T.: Could we try and capture the greatness of Gandhiji? In what does it reside?

A.P.J.: Gandhiji was primarily responsible for the transformation of the demand for independence into a nationwide mass movement that mobilized every class of society against the imperialist forces, yet the free India that came into being, divided and committed to a program of modernization and industrialization, was not the India of his dreams.

A.T.: During the independence struggle, many Indian scientists rose to glory and international acclaim. Did they also shape the Indian psyche?

A.P.J.: It is not a question of psyche alone, which they certainly shaped; they indeed laid the foundation of an identity on which the modern nation was built, of course in tandem with political effort. They gave the people of India tremendous confidence.

A.T.: There was a period, 20-30 years, of spectacular rise of Indian science.

A.P.J.: You are right. During 1920-40 almost parallel to the political and social awakening, Indian science also was stimulated. Jagdish Chandra Bose, C.V. Raman, M. Visvesvaraya, Meghnath Saha, Srinivasa Ramanujan, Subrahmanyan Chandrasekhar, so many brilliant minds enlightened Indian nationalism.

A.T.: Who, in particular, inspired you?

A.P.J.: Though I admire them all, I am particularly inspired by Srinivasa Ramanujan. I shared with him a humble beginning. My father was a boat-man, his father worked as a clerk in a cloth merchant's shop. Both were actually blessed by the power of the Almighty. But the similarity ends there. While I was a run-of-the-mill student, by age twelve Ramanujan had mastered trigonometry so completely that he was inventing sophisticated theorems that astonished his teachers.

A.T.: Robert Kanigel[72] writes in *The Man Who Knew Infinity* that Ramanujan could envision unique mathematical concepts just as ordinary people see the waves in an ocean.

A.P.J.: Ironically, his focus on math became his academic undoing. He outpaced his teachers in the theory of numbers, but neglected all other subjects. He could speak adequate English, but failed in it and history, and other science courses.

A.T.: And then the providential break came. Ramanujan wrote a simple letter to the renowned G.H. Hardy at Cambridge University enclosing one hundred of his theorem equations. In Kanigel's words, "A single look at them was enough to show that they could only be written down by a mathematician of the highest class. They must be true, for if they were not true, no one would have the imagination to invent them."

A.P.J.: Arun, You seem to have read quite a bit on Ramanujan?

A.T.: Working with you has never been easy. Many interesting things are written about Ramanujan. There are several anecdotes too, almost making a myth out of his mental landscape.

A.P.J.: Tell me one.

A.T.: Once Ramanujan had fallen seriously ill and was convalescing in a country house. Hardy took a taxi to visit him. As math masters like to do he noted the taxi's number – 1729 – to see if it yielded any interesting permutations. To him it didn't and he thought as he went up the steps to the door, that it was a rather dull number and hoped it was not an inauspicious sign. He mentioned 1729 to Ramanujan who immediately countered, "Actually, it is a very interesting number. It is the smallest number expressible as the sum of two cubes in two different ways."[73]

A.P.J.: What are these numbers?

A.T.: These are the cubes of 1 and 12 and cubes of 9 and 10. Both, when added become 1729.

A.T.: What aspect touches you deepest about Ramanujan?

A.P.J.: While Ramanujan's work reflects his true genius, his life also highlights the miseries associated with the rural middle class and the poor in this country. He was only thirty-three at the time of his death.

A.T.: Is there a design at work? Genius suffers everywhere.

A.P.J.: I really don't know. But what I can say for sure is that pain often includes a godly component of soulful satisfaction and it surely has spiritual meaning. Certain energies come only when you burn.

A.T.: Coming back to the sudden burst of scientific genius in India, how do you relate it to the world as it was at that time?

A.P.J.: A significant event happened in 1893. A ship called *Empress of India* sailed from Yokohama in Japan to Vancouver in Canada. On board were two extraordinary Indians—Swami Vivekananda and Jamsetji N. Tata. Both were headed for Chicago on two different missions. Swamiji was to attend the World Congress of Religions. Jamsetji was going to see World's Columbian Exposition, a celebration of technology and industrial progress. On board the ship, Jamsetji discussed his plans to start a steel mill in India. Swamiji told Jamsetji that there were two parts to the challenge—manufacturing technology and the science of steel. The technology could be brought from abroad but the science had to be researched at home. This seeded the idea in Jamsetji Tata's mind to start the Indian Institute of Science at Bangalore.

He later wrote to Swamiji in 1898, asking for his support for the venture.

A.T.: I have seen the facsimile of that historical letter. The exact words Jamsetji Tata used were: "I know not who would make a more fitting general of such a campaign than Vivekananda." Swamiji in turn wrote, "I am not aware if any project, at once so opportune and so far reaching in its beneficent effects, has ever been mooted in India...The scheme grasps the vital point of weakness in our national well-being with a clearness of vision and tightness of grip, the mastery of which is only equalled by the munificence of the gift that is being ushered to the public."[74]

A.P.J.: Swamiji passed away in 1902. The splendid Indian Institute of Science eventually started functioning in Bangalore in 1909.

A.T.: So, India was ushered into the twentieth century on an orderly note.

A.P.J.: Well, the century started with the 'Wright Brothers' triumph over wind. Then in 1905, a year often referred to as the Miracle Year, Albert Einstein published five papers on three major subjects, namely, Theory of Relativity, Photoelectric Effect and Brownian Motion. In India, C.V. Raman took off during that time.

A.T.: We saw a spectacular surge of thought at once, so to say. Almost 2,500 years ago, Buddha, Socrates and Confucius all appeared simultaneously in different parts of the world, talking about reason and rationality.

A.P.J.: What a coincidence!

A.T.: At the time of Raman's youth, what were the sorts of opportunities that aspiring scientists in India had?

A.P.J.: Well, there was nothing. This forced C.V. Raman to accept a position with the Indian Civil Services as an Assistant Accountant General in Calcutta. While he was there, he was able to sustain his interest in science by working, in his spare time, in the laboratories of the Indian Association for the Cultivation of Science.

A.T.: In *Journey Into Light*, G. Venkataraman writes that in 1917, with his scientific standing established in India, Raman was offered the position of Professor of Physics at Calcutta University, where he stayed for the next fifteen years. During his tenure there, he received worldwide recognition for his work in optics and the scattering of light.

A.P.J.: Incidentally, G. Venkataraman is a dear friend of mine. We worked together in DRDO[75]. I vividly remember his fascinating account of the birth of the idea of the famous Raman Effect.

A.T.: Yes Sir. In 1921, The Universities of the British Empire met in London, and Raman went on his first visit abroad as the representative of Calcutta University. On his return journey, as he enjoyed the magnificent beauty of the vast Mediterranean Sea around him, he wondered: Is the sea blue due to the reflection of the blue sky? Yet even when big waves rolled over the surface, the colour did not change and remained blue. Lost in his caravan of thoughts as the ship glided through the expanse of water, an idea flashed in his mind's eye. Could it be that water molecules are scattering the sunlight, causing the blue colour? He was possessed by this idea and barely a month after his return, sent a research paper to the Royal Society of London. Within a year, he published a detailed article on the molecular scattering of light. In 1924, he was elected to the Royal Society of London.

A.P.J.: Tell me more about it.

A.T.: G. Venkataraman points out that Newton had earlier showed in his famous prism experiment that light is made up of countless colours. Using a prism, Newton dispersed light into a spectrum of colours. But Raman's research was focused on what happens when one such monochromatic light beam passes through a transparent substance, like water, for instance. Naturally, the beam scatters in random directions, but one tiny part of the scattered light changes its frequency from that of the initial colour. It results from a molecule changing its molecular motion. In February 1928, C.V. Raman finally observed two low-intensity spectral lines that confirmed this theory. The phenomenon was called the Raman Effect. The inelastically scattered light was called the Raman Scatter. The British made him a Knight of the British Empire in 1929 and in 1930, for the first time in its history, an Indian scholar, educated entirely in India, had received the highest honour in science, the Nobel Prize in Physics.[76]

A.P.J.: So remarkable it was. So gratifying to hear!

Knowing molecular changes by observing the Raman Scatter, science acquired a powerful tool.

A.T.: Within the first twelve years of discovery of Raman Effect, about 1,800 research papers were published and about 2,500 chemical compounds were studied by researchers and scientists around the world. These included pure water, vapours, gases, crystals, quartz, ice and even alcohol. Derek A. Long wrote very comprehensively about it all in *The Raman Effect*.

A.P.J.: And then he came to Bangalore.

A.T.: Yes Sir. From 1933 till 1970, when he passed away, he lived and worked in Bangalore, first at the Indian Institute of Science and then his own Raman Research Institute.

A.P.J.: The Raman Research Institute was founded in 1948 out of private funds. The main activity of the institute was basic research in selected areas of physics which were of particular interest to C.V. Raman. The Institute trained excellent scientists in the areas of Astronomy and Astrophysics, Liquid Crystals, Theoretical Physics and Optics.

A.T.: Satish Dhawan remained associated with the Raman Institute till his last days.

A.P.J.: Blessed are these great souls. I always tell young students this story of Sir C.V. Raman:

A research student of Physics was conducting an experiment with 1 kilowatt power X-ray tube. On hearing that a scientist in England was experimenting on the same problem with a 5 kilowatt X-ray tube, he grew dejected. When C.V. Raman got to know of this, he walked up to the student and with a smile said: "There is a very simple solution, use a 10 kilowatt brain only on the problem."[77]

He was speaking from experience. You know, he had won the Nobel Prize for Physics with simple equipment he built personally without any grant or external funding.

A.T.: So hard to believe. Would you elaborate on any particular aspect of his great life and thought, which inspired you?

A.P.J.: Raman laid the foundation for industrial science. Seven decades down the line, Silicon lasers and optical amplifiers based on the Raman Effect have opened up new photonic possibilities for silicon data amplifiers, wavelength converters and icon deployment. In what could disrupt the photonics space, Intel Corporation has developed the world's first silicon-based continuous-wave laser on a single chip—built around Raman Effect.

A.T.: You identify deeply with Raman's reverence for nature.

A.P.J.: Raman called Nature the Supreme artist. Nature creates forms of beauty, loveliness and colour, unsurpassable and this has been so from the beginning of time. She is the source of inspiration of not only artists, painters, sculptors and engineers, but also of men of science. All you have to do is to go around with a basket of gratitude and receive the bounty.

A.T.: Amongst all the people, who left the deepest imprints on you?
A.P.J.: Very simple. My mother! And I suppose this is true for all of us.

A.T.: Well Sir, I can so easily recall from *Wings of Fire* that your mother Ashiamma was born in an affluent Tamil Muslim family. One of her forebears had been bestowed the title of *Bahadur* by the British. She married your father Jainulabdeen, at the age of 25, a tall, well-built man who lived on the Rameswaram Island. Your father had neither much formal education nor much wealth. She bore him five children, you being the youngest.

A.P.J.: You are a good guy! When I look back at my childhood, a beautiful kaleidoscope of good human values, simple and joyous people, sea waves, hovering seagulls, golden sand, a crowd of faithful pilgrims arriving from distant places, the Mosque Street, prayers, school, petty shops, horse carts emerge. Everything then merges into the figure of one graceful pious lady—my mother Ashiamma.

A.T.: Tell me more.
A.P.J.: My childhood was quite comfortable in the sense that my parents, absorbing all problems, provided us with all the basic amenities—shelter, food, clothing, education and above all, a loving environment. During World War-II, however, there was scarcity all around presenting challenge and toil. I would get up quite early in the morning and watch my parents offer their *Fajr* (daybreak) prayer. Even before the Sun

arose from the blue waters of the sea, my father would go to a coconut grove he owned about four miles from our house. I would walk many miles to the house of my saintly teacher. I would also attend an Arabic school.

A.T.: But then, when would you do your newspaper business?

A.P.J.: After the two learning sessions, I would collect newspapers at the Station and go door-to-door distributing them for my cousin, who would pay me an *anna* for this effort.

A.T.: And what would you do with that money?

A.P.J.: I would proudly take the coin to my mother and deposit it with her. I didn't ever need that money, but when I had to go to Ramanathapuram for my high school education, my mother produced all the coins, now a significant amount, she had so jealously treasured. Tears welled in my eyes. She ran her fingers through my hair and quietly said—"Son, mothers only give."

A.T.: Yes Sir, mothers only give. I too was very fortunate in that sense.

A.P.J.: Tell me about your mother?

A.T.: She went for teachers' training, looking after four children and my grandmother, to augment the modest salary of my father. It was a great struggle. She indeed gave wings to me.

A.P.J.: As your mother gave, my mother gave, all mothers

give. The day would be spent at school. In the evenings, I would help my cousin run his small shop and return late. My mother would be waiting with supper ready. Normally we used to be the last to eat. Sitting on the floor of the kitchen, she would place a banana leaf before me, on which she would then serve hot white rice, fresh coconut chutney, spicy home-made pickles and *sambar*.

I would then read in the night by lantern-light. Every night—after washing the dishes, sweeping the floor, and preparing rice for tomorrow's meal—my mother would spread clean mattresses for all of us children, give us kisses with a short prayer.

A.T.: In the poem 'My Mother' in *Wings of Fire* you recount your illness. When did that happen?

A.P.J.: When I was ten years old I had high fever, suffered for many days, and was in great pain. My mother, like an angel, would hover around me, caressing me with her 'feathers'. Her gentle and caring touch cooled down the ferocity of the fever and I recovered speedily.

A.T.: Please tell me something you have not shared with me in the past.

A.P.J.: Well, in 1952, when I was studying at St. Joseph's College, Trichurapalli. One summer afternoon when I was at home during the vacation, I asked my mother, "Tell me what my father was like when he was about my age?" My mother stopped her sewing and looked up, surprised at my question. After what seemed like a long-time she answered, "He was never like you. He never dreamed of being a lawyer, professor, or anything, other than a husband, father and grandfather. You were the youngest of our five children, and every waking moment was filled with work and responsibilities to feed and clothe the family. On this island, there was only one career for him, and that was being a hard-working man. People loved him for his pious demeanour." I felt a bit humbled. I thought I was doing great work studying science in a far-off city pursuing a career that would take me places. And here was my mother, revering the simple, anchored life of my father.

A.T.: Blessed are such couples.
A.P.J.: May peace be upon them.

A.T.: Tell me more about the people around the neighbourhood.
A.P.J.: At Rameswaram, like most other people, my parents lived with their family in a community whose economy was based on marine products—fish and shells—the business of providing basic services and provisions to the pilgrims and selling artefacts. They never thought of leaving their homeland, migrating to cities, and ending up as one of the thousands of people living in Madurai, Trichurapalli, Madras and even Sri Lanka, at that time called Ceylon. My parents had contributed little to the world through their simple lives but so valiantly held on to certain sound and noble traditions, when tested by the turbulence and viciousness of life.

A.T.: How would you explain this?

A.P.J.: My mother symbolised a culture where honour, respect and family solidarity took precedence over individual desires. "Men are important," my mother would tell me when I asked her why she always ate last at all meal times. "Men are stronger and wiser—therefore, they always eat before women. And anyway, more than my own meal, I enjoy seeing all of you eat." Even today when I eat alone in the Rashtrapati Bhavan, I can feel my mother watching me, sitting by my side, holding a handmade fan in her hand and gently fanning me with it.

A.T.: What do you feel had the most profound impact on your soul?

A.P.J.: The devotion of my parents for each other—the mutual respect. That summer afternoon of 1952, I sat in silence as I listened to my mother. I hated seeing my father work tirelessly and my mother always saddled with household chores, as I was growing up. They worked so hard to provide simple things of life to all of us and many others in the extended family, even neighbours and distant relatives. Once I asked my mother—I saw you working without respite the whole day in the house and every night. Not once did my father said anything equivalent of thank you or something like, "Ashia, you're a good wife." Did it not hurt you?

She stared out of the window, remembering how I grew up. "Your father was a great man. He never wanted anything for himself. He only provided for others. Giving was central to his life." My mother looked down at her sewing and continued. "Nothing of me was ever unimportant for your father. I was so very glad to leave the comforts of my parents' house when I married your father. Well, it's too late to tell him now and he wouldn't understand anyway. And I know he always knew it, even if he never said so. If he didn't, he wouldn't have cared to ask me before taking any decision. He always cared for my opinion. He made me a part of his own self. Where is the space for words and gestures my dear son Abul?"

Growing up, my mother had never initiated a serious conversation with me. It was always a few passing comments about my careless attitude, shabby clothes and hairstyle; about how I'd have to control my anger and my thirst for knowledge in order to be a good and modest man. Through generations dedicated to bringing up children within their meagre resources, Indian women had taught their daughters and sons what they needed to survive: how to cook, clean, haul water and stitch; how to be productive, obedient, respectful and patient.

I saw my mother caring for my aged and sick father as the most skilled and caring nurse would do. When my father breathed his last in 1976, I sat with my mother for a long-time in silence. She perhaps wanted to tell me something that no son would be prepared to listen—that her mission on this planet was over. I knew that though I would be the happiest person to take her to Thumba and keep her under great care and medical attention, she would never agree to that. She always visualized herself as the custodian of her husband Jainulabdeen's tribe for whom she was always a giving and caring soul. That was my last meeting with her body. She passed away a few months later and I came from Thumba for the burial.

A.T.: Do you miss her?
A.P.J.: I never lost her.

A.T.: Suppose she is sitting here, in this Immortal Hut, under this great Banyan Tree, what would she say?
A.P.J.: My mother would say, "Yes, I have many children, and I love them all. But you are my youngest child, the best in everything to me, my last hope of seeing my blood excelled. I've been very strict and hard on you, but I raised you in the only way I knew. I am proud of you."

A.T.: And how would you respond?
A.P.J.: "My mother! I would have disappointed you on many occasions and on many counts, but I have always tried not to let you down on your piety or undermine your nobility. I am proud of you too."

A.T.: Can you tell me about any other woman whom you have admired?
A.P.J.: I have always admired with respect M.S. Subbulakshmi. She was an extremely traditional and conservative woman of her generation. I bathe my soul in her music.

A.T.: What do you think is so special in her music?
A.P.J.: Subbulakshmi's virtuosity in rhythm-charged

ragam—tanam-pallavi techniques is sublime. She immortalized pallavi in Raga Begada, "*Kailasapate, pasupate, umapate, namostute*," across the Adi tala cycle. You reach at such a stage through dedication, toil and years of continuous practice. She was the face and voice of the Carnatic music.[78] For the last five decades, I have been waking up to a new day listening to her rendering of the *Venkateswara Suprabhatam*, a *bhakti geet*.

A.T.: Other than her music, what are the other attributes in her that inspired you the most?

A.P.J.: Her simplicity. Fame and the adoration of thousands of fans left Subbulakshmi untouched. To the very end, she remained the simple, neat, devout, down to earth person she always was, with a genuine interest in others.

A.T.: Music gave her soul-growth.

A.P.J.: Subbulakshmi is an inspiring role model, not simply in terms of aesthetic and cultural refinement but for some of her sterling qualities: humility, compassion, consideration for others and unwavering principles of conduct.

A.T.: Alexis Carrel[79] said, "Prayer, like radium, is a luminous and self-generating form of energy."

A.P.J.: Witnessing M.S. singing with her eyes closed, the final notes—*'Kurai onrum illai'* (Lord, I have no regrets); I feel that the Universe holds nothing back from the one who lovingly and sincerely gives.

A.T.: Coming back to the world of power politics, whom do you relate to most?

A.P.J.: Like people in South Africa revere Gandhiji, I admire Nelson Mandela.

A.T.: You went to South Africa in September 2004.

A.P.J.: Anyone who travels over the vast expanse of South Africa is immediately struck by the great variations in its landscape and the differing contexts and conditions under which rural people live. Indian and South African people share a common history of land dispossession and the manner in which European settlers accumulated capital and laid the foundations for their own well-being at the expense of the indigenous people.

A.T.: I have read that in 1652 Europeans settled where Cape Town is now located, to set up a half-way station for ships travelling to the East. Early European records describe these pastoralists, with large herds of stock, as being far wealthier than the average European peasant of the time. However, their wealth and prosperity would prove short-lived in the face of more, increasingly aggressive European migration into the interior.

A.P.J.: It is truer in the Indian context.

A.T.: The expansion of the Cape colony was, however, not a smooth or uncontested process – African people consistently resisted the dispossession of their territory. During the 17th, 18th and most of the 19th century there was ongoing conflict between settlers and indigenous people. Forms of resistance differed – from raids on settler livestock to protracted periods of guerrilla resistance and open warfare. Resistance was ruthlessly crushed – initially by armed commandos (comprising European farmers, slaves and African vassals) and later, from 1811, by the British army.

A.P.J.: I was told during my visit that the struggle to resist land dispossession and the systematic subjugation of indigenous people has been a long and bitter one. Africans fought fiercely to protect their land and defend their livelihoods and their way of life. Resistance took many forms, from outright war to events such as cattle-killings. Stories of the heroic struggles of Makana, Sirhili, Mhlontlo, Sigcawu, Cetywayo and Bambata have been handed down from generation to generation. Many of these leaders were captured and imprisoned on Robben Island or in the dungeons of the Cape Town Castle, others died in battle.

A.T.: The issue of land has always featured on the liberation agenda in South Africa. The Freedom Charter demanded: "The land should be shared amongst those who work it" and reflected many of the concerns of the rural poor, as did the manifestos of all other political organisations. In a similar situation in India, however, the same can't be said.

A.P.J.: It is very important that land reforms are implemented into a wider rural development and agrarian reform strategy.

A.T.: In *Long walk to Freedom*, Nelson Mandela provides details of his childhood. Born on 18 July,

1918 in Umtata and named Rolihlahla Mandela, he spent his early childhood in the Transkei, on the Eastern Coast of South Africa. He educated himself in law.

A.P.J.: Tell me more about him.

A.T.: Steven Mufson[80] in *Fighting Years* provides an account of the events at the height of World War-II, when a small group of young Africans, members of the African National Congress (ANC), banded together. Starting out with a 60-member group, these young people set themselves the formidable task of transforming the ANC into a mass movement, deriving its strength and motivation from the unlettered millions of working people in the towns and countryside.

In 1952, Nelson Mandela was given the responsibility to prepare an organisational plan that would enable the leadership of the movement to maintain dynamic contact with its membership without recourse to public meetings. Mandela built up powerful local and regional branches and devolved the political power. He opened the first black legal partnership in the country.

A.P.J.: I can see the template of Gandhiji.

A.T.: In a biography of Mandela, Anthony Sampson[81] writes that during the whole of the fifties, he was the victim of various forms of repression. Mandela was banned, arrested and imprisoned. He was made one of the accused in the mammoth Treason Trial, at great cost to his legal practice and his political work. The Trial eventually collapsed in 1961 and South Africa was steered towards the adoption of the republic constitution. However, soon Mandela was sentenced to life imprisonment and lodged in the notorious Robben Island, a maximum security prison, 7 km off the coast near Cape Town.

A.P.J.: I visited Robben Island. I was told that Mandela organised political education classes there, virtually turning it into a centre for learning. It was here that Mandela told his tormentors, "Any man or institution that tries to rob me of my dignity will lose." Mandela's major response to the indignities of the prison was a creative denial of victimhood, expressed most remarkably by a system of self-education, which earned the prison the appellation of 'Island University'.

A.T.: Andre Brink[82] wrote in *Time 100*, "When in February 1990, President F.W. de Klerk lifted the ban on the ANC, the real test of Mandela began. Every inch of the way, Mandela had to win the support of his own followers. More difficult still was the process of allaying white fears. But the patience, the wisdom, the visionary quality Mandela brought to his struggle, and above all the moral integrity with which he set about to unify a divided people, resulted in the country's first democratic elections and his selection as President.

Tormented by the scandals that pursued his wife Winnie, from whom he finally parted; plagued by corruption among his followers; dogged by worries about delivering on programs of job creation and housing in a country devastated by White greed, he has become a sadder, wiser man."

A.P.J.: Mandela indeed was a great teacher of life. His Presidency saw an unprecedented Truth and Reconciliation exercise. With the influential help of Bishop Desmond Tutu, Mandela brought the oppressors and the oppressed in front of each other and let forgiveness emerge. Mandela refused to counter racism with racism. His life has been an inspiration, in South Africa and elsewhere to those who are oppressed and deprived, and to all who are opposed to oppression and deprivation.

A.T.: Mandela said: "Let us recall how we emerged from a conflict that threatened to have this country rendered a piece of scorched Earth and its cities flowing with streets of blood. We averted all that through a common commitment to a new observance of the human dignity of each other irrespective of racial, religious, cultural or other differences. Let us in this venture too remain true to that commitment to human dignity and equality of all."[83]

A.P.J.: Mandela's life symbolises the triumph of the human spirit over man's inhumanity to man. He personifies struggle. Let no one doubt it: People like Mandela are ready to die for certain ideals and they are even more determined to live for their realization for all.

A.T.: Nelson Mandela received the Nobel Peace Prize in 1993 on behalf of all South Africans who suffered and sacrificed so much to bring peace to their land.

A.P.J.: How exemplary that he sacrificed his private life and his youth for his people, for a noble cause!

A.T.: What is the message?

A.P.J.: Mandela demonstrated that we remain locked in an undeveloped and underdeveloped version of ourselves only if we persist in closing our minds and hearts to the Universal pain around us. Mandela not only broke the jug, he bathed in the river.

A.T.: Ralph Waldo Emerson[84] said, "True peace is a quality you carry within yourself, regardless of external circumstances." "Can anything be so elegant as to have few wants, and to serve them oneself?" Emerson asks.

A.P.J.: Mandela lived these words. When I shook hand with Nelson Mandela, I felt that I am touching a mighty soul. He was moving with a walking stick. After shaking hand with me, he discarded the walking stick and walked holding my hand; I became his support. A big lesson that we learnt from the great personality of Nelson Mandela is explained by Thiruvalluvar:

> tiraṉalla tarpirar ceyyiṉum nōnontu
> araṉalla ceyyāmai naṉṟu.
>
> For those who do ill to you,
> the best punishment is to return good to them.[85]

Nelson Mandela opened his soul to the pain of his people and the most dreaded prison failed to shackle his indomitable spirit. I see him as one of the great moral and political leaders of our time.

A.T.: May I now come to your own career. You have written about Vikram Sarabhai, Homi Jehangir Bhabha, Satish Dawan, Brahm Prakash, D.S. Kothari, Raja Ramanna...Who amongst these great souls impressed you or touched you the most?

A.P.J.: Everyone is a unique scientist. However, I worked under Satish Dhawan directly for a decade. Vikram Sarabhai is our revered Guru as a visionary.

A.T.: I met Satish Dhawan in 1990, when he gave a lecture on *The Flight of Birds*, in Hyderabad. You introduced him to the audience with a reverence that was so real.

A.P.J.: What impressed me most about a Dhawan was his versatility. At various times in his career, he had been a teacher, research scientist, engineer, technologist, manager, leader and adviser – sometimes many of these at the same time. And to everything he did, he brought dedication, breadth of vision, meticulousness and humanity, which combined with his remarkable scientific and technological abilities, transformed every single organisation he worked for or led, and made it achieve what it had often not thought itself capable of.

A.T.: I have read R. Ramachandran's article about Satish Dhawan in *Frontline*[86]. Satish Dhawan was born in Srinagar. He graduated from the University of Punjab (Lahore) with an unusual combination of degrees: a B.A. in Mathematics and Physics, an M.A. in English Literature, and a B.E. in Mechanical Engineering. In 1947, he obtained an M.S. in Aeronautical

Engineering from the University of Minnesota, and moved to the California Institute of Technology, where he was awarded the Aeronautical Engineer's Degree in 1949 and a Ph.D. in Aeronautics and Mathematics in 1951 with Hans W. Liepmann, an eminent aerospace scientist and authority in fluid dynamics. What a magnificent sweep!

A.P.J.: The great educational breadth, covering science, engineering and the humanities and his distinguished family background, appear to have given Satish Dhawan an ability to view the world from many different angles, and may explain in part his unique qualities as a leader.

A.T.: Roddam Narasimha captured Satish Dhawan's life very well in the obituary he wrote[87]. At the time when Dhawan began his career in aerodynamic research, supersonic flows and shock waves were still rather exotic phenomena; his earliest papers dealt with these subjects and one of them, which had detailed observations of how a shock wave bounces off a solid surface (such as that of a wing, for example) became widely known for its revealing and defining observations. Satish Dhawan invented an ingenious method of directly measuring the friction drag on a surface. These results appeared in various books of the time, including Schlichting's *Boundary Layer Theory.* They have faithfully reproduced Satish Dhawan's work in the many editions the book has gone through over the last fifty years, including the eighth print in 1999.

A.P.J.: Roddam Narasimha writes very well.

A.T.: Roddam Narasimha remembered him as a tall, handsome, young man who would jump out of his sporty little MG car, wearing a red shirt and a broad smile, racing across the staircase in the Department and cheerfully saying 'Good morning' as he stepped into the classroom. He brought to the Institute an element of youth, freshness, modernity, earnestness and informality that captivated his students and many colleagues. Singular and very visible, he was a star on the campus. His sense of humour and his socialistic leanings added to make a personality that many found irresistible.

A.P.J.: I have some very fond memories of Dhawan. So I would like to talk about Dhawan's inner space.

A.T.: What a beautiful aspect!

A.P.J.: There were two outstanding features of Dhawan's philosophy in research. First, it was carried out at low cost, with ingenious development or adaptation of whatever materials, skills and instrumentation were available at the time; second, the basic research areas investigated in his laboratories were all inspired in some way by the problems faced by the newly-born aircraft industry of the country. Dhawan constantly sought to promote the development of this industry at the higher levels of policy and management.

A.T.: When did you start interacting with Dhawan?

A.P.J.: During 1959-61, I was at the Aeronautical Development Establishment (ADE) in Bangalore. We were designing the Hovercraft Nandi. One of the typical design problems of Hovercraft was the design of a contra rotating propeller. I knew how to design a propeller, but I had no clue about the design of a contra rotating one that involves taking into account the duct effect. I asked O.P. Mediratta, the then Director of ADE, whether I could seek the help of Dhawan for this design, since my friends had told me about his great teaching abilities. He agreed and I went to I.I.Sc. (Indian Institute of Sciences). When I asked Satish Dhawan for help in the design, he said he would teach me how to design a contra rotating propeller, but that I would have to come to him for ten Saturdays from 2 to 3 o'clock in the afternoon. It was a great teacher's offer. I was jubilant and started attending the one-to-one classes. He taught me how to design it. After the first lecture, before beginning the second one, he asked me very critical questions pertaining to the first lecture. He tested the degree of my assimilation and the potential I apparently had for the application of this understanding. With this background, I attended all the ten lectures. At the end of these sessions, I felt confident enough to take up the task of designing the contra rotating propeller.

A.T.: How did Satish Dhawan reach ISRO?

A.P.J.: In 1972, Satish Dhawan was appointed Chairman of the Space Commission and of the Indian Space Research Organisation, and Secretary to the Government of India in the Department of Space. It was an appointment that served as a tremendous source of inspiration to many.

A.T.: I don't mean to compare the two, both of whom are legends, but how do you look back at the contributions of Sarabhai and Dhawan?

A.P.J.: The Indian Space Programme owes its birth to the vision of Vikram Sarabhai who had envisioned India building and launching satellites, which would provide beneficial applications such as remote sensing, meteorology, communications and direct TV broadcasting. He shaped the Space Programme, giving it the organisational structure and management methods which have made it one of the most dynamic and successful institutions. But the superb technology development organisation, ISRO is the loving creation of Satish Dhawan.

A.T.: Any special memory you cherish?

A.P.J.: In 1980, we were discussing space missions for the next two decades at the ISRO Headquarters in Bangalore. Many mission options were debated. The next morning Dhawan summarised the entire discussions with charts prepared in his own hand. These charts became the blueprints for the National Space Programme for the next 15 years including launch vehicles for Polar and Geostationary Satellites (PSLV and GSLV), the Indian Remote Sensing Satellites, the INSAT series, and their current technological variants.

A.T.: You showed me the copies of those charts. You treasure them as if they were sacred leaves of scriptures.

A.P.J.: Another great memory I have of Dhawan is about

his leadership strength. He unfailingly took the responsibility when there were failures, but generously gave credit to others when there were successes. When the maiden launch of SLV-3, on 10 August, 1979, failed under my mission control, he faced the gruelling media himself. He announced, "Friends, today we had launched our first satellite launch vehicle to place a satellite in orbit, but we could not succeed. It is our first mission of proving multiple technologies in satellite and satellite launch vehicles. In many technologies we have succeeded and in a few more we have yet to succeed. Above all, I realise my team members have to be given more on the technological support. I am going to do that and the next mission will succeed."

But when the second launch successfully put Rohini Satellite in orbit, on 18 July, 1980, Satish Dhawan put me forward in the glare.

A.T.: Any particular leadership trait we can identify with Satish Dhawan?

A.P.J.: I think yes. Most of the scientific organisations suffer in properly assessing the individual contributions. And it is indeed never an easy task. Satish Dhawan maintained accountability through peer pressure, but in honest failures shielded his engineers from criticism. He developed a promotion and assessment system that enabled the more productive engineers to move ahead of their colleagues retaining the confidence of the peers in the fairness of the system.

A.T.: And how did he handle the top?

A.P.J.: He insisted, successfully, that the National Space Programme should be a purely civilian enterprise.

A.T.: As a guiding soul, how do we describe him?

A.P.J.: The citation presented to him when he was awarded the 1999 Indira Gandhi Award for National Integration brings out well his essence: "one of our foremost scientists, teachers and nation builders... he made multi-dimensional contributions to scientific education, research, policy formulation and implementation, and is deeply concerned with the solution of national problems through the use of science..."

A.T.: There is so much glory in what scientists do, but there are immeasurable hardships that lie beneath. Do you feel they get a raw deal when it comes to worldly rewards?

A.P.J.: Well, it is a question of perceptions. But I would like to cite the example of Einstein here. After World War-II, Einstein was a leading figure in the world government movement.

A.T.: I understand Einstein was offered the Presidency of the State of Israel which he declined.

A.P.J.: He played a key role in establishing the Hebrew University of Jerusalem. During 1921, Einstein made his first visit to the United States primarily to raise funds for his dream University.[88] Einstein's gifts inevitably resulted in his dwelling much in intellectual solitude.

A.T.: Is intellectual solitude essential?
A.P.J.: Perhaps yes.

A.T.: Sir, I have read that music played an important part in Einstein's life. Raja Ramanna's dexterity on Piano and your interest in Veena are well-known.
A.P.J.: See, music is the best prescription for relaxation. It just cleans you up from the inner side.

A.T.: Let us go Sir, to a tough terrain.
A.P.J.: What is that?

A.T.: In the foreword of *Markings* by Dag Hammarskjold[89], W.H. Auden[90] writes that it is easy to look at greatness from a distance—to speak of some great person who might have lived years or centuries ago. The tough part is to see and recognize greatness around you, in your own time. Would you like to mention a guiding soul who is still around in flesh and blood?

A.P.J.: I will certainly do that. But before that I would like you to understand a few aspects of guiding souls.

A.T.: Sir!
A.P.J.: Guiding souls are the luckiest of mortals because what they must do is the same as what they most want to do. They are so certain that their work is good and will stand the test of time that even if their genius goes unrecognized in their life-time, they always enjoy the earthly reward of satisfaction of a job well done.

A.T.: So, they don't need posterity to celebrate their achievements. In a sense, they would have had their reward in their lives itself.

A.P.J.: They are so engaged in their spiritual work that this world runs after them. They live in the *Kingdom of Heaven* right here. In a manner in which Verghese Kurien lives in Anand.

A.T.: Sir, I had been to the Milkman's abode. Verghese Kurien not only built one of the largest and most successful institutions in India—Amul; this model of cooperative dairy development engineered the White Revolution in India and made India the largest milk producer in the world.

A.P.J.: So tell me what you know about Kurien.

A.T.: Sir, I have read M.V. Kamath's *Milkman from Anand: The story of Verghese Kurien.* He graduated from Loyola College, Madras in 1940 and then did B.E. in Mechanical Engineering from the Madras University. He started his career with Tata Steel and Technical Institute, Jamshedpur but later went to USA to pursue his Masters in Mechanical Engineering from Michigan State University. In 1949, when Kurien returned, he was posted as a Dairy Engineer at the government creamery in Anand. Around the same time, the infant cooperative dairy, Kaira District Cooperative Milk Producers' Union was fighting a battle with Polson Dairy, a multinational company. Inspired by Sardar Vallabhbhai Patel, who said that if the farmers of India are to get economic freedom, then they must get out of the clutches of the middlemen, young Kurien joined hands with the social leader Tribhuvandas Patel to set up a dairy processing plant.

A.P.J.: And how did the brand name Amul come?

A.T.: The book says that Amul comes from the Sanskrit word—*Amoolya*, meaning priceless. It was suggested by a quality control expert working in Anand. The first products with this brand name were launched in 1955. Since then, they have been in use in millions of homes in all parts of India and abroad. Today Amul is a symbol of high quality products sold at reasonable prices and available everywhere.

A.P.J.: I recently received Amul buttermilk sent by Kurien. It has a very long shelf-life. I feel that there is something more that makes the Amul brand special. Amul is the brand name of two million farmers, members of 10,000 village dairy cooperative societies throughout Gujarat.

A.T.: What else do you see in Amul?

A.P.J.: The essence of Kurien manifested in the success of the Amul – *The taste of India*. It found expression in a larger than life purpose. Amul's purpose is freedom to farmers by giving total control over procurement, production and marketing. Amrita Patel[91] is now ably leading the mission.

A.T.: Sir, Norman E. Borlaug[92] says in the foreword of *An Unfinished Dream* that he considers Verghese Kurien to be one of the world's great agricultural leaders of this century. Kurien's work can help to light the way for those who must carry on the battle to ensure greater food security, prosperity and peace to the world.

A.P.J.: Beautiful words!

A.T.: Verghese Kurien heads the Viksit Bharat (Developed India) Trust created to carry out pilot scale societal projects aimed at transforming rural India. You donated part of the retirement money that you received from the life-long service of the Government of India to this Trust.

A.P.J.: Be grateful as your deeds become less and less associated with your name.

A.T.: In the post-independence phase of Indian science, who were the most influential figures?

A.P.J.: I would like to mention D.S. Kothari[93], Homi Bhabha and Vikram Sarabhai. These three physicists went on to build huge science and technology institutions that eventually became a home for more than 20,000 young scientists and engineers and kindled their innovativeness.

A.T.: They chose to stay back in India.

A.P.J.: I believe that if these three great scientists had gone on to concentrate only on physics, at least one of them would have got the Nobel Prize, but India would not have had the advantage of having atomic energy, space and defence research organisations in the country of this scale and magnitude. To me, these great organisations are our Nobel Prizes.

A.T.: Building organisations, particularly in the developing countries, is very important.
A.P.J.: Look at the effort of my friend Kakarla Subbarao in the area of healthcare.

A.T.: You said admirable words about him in the historic session of Andhra Pradesh Legislative Assembly on 11 July, 2004
A.P.J.: I declared Kakarla's righteousness in the right congregation.

A.T.: You said, "You would like to recall a great human Kakarla Subbarao. The more you understood his life, the more you were inspired. He brought tertiary health care to India. His own house has been transformed into a school. He was the founder Director of the Nizam's Institute of Medical Sciences (NIMS) and a radiologist of international acclaim. He has been declared as the Indian Radiologist of the millennium by his peers. Many doctors today throughout the country are his students serving in a number of hospitals. With him, you conducted many camps in tribal villages for cancer diagnosis and brought patients to the city for treatment."
A.P.J.: Good memory.

A.T.: Sir, I wrote the autobiographical work—*A Doctor's Story of Life and Death*, with Kakarla Subbarao. It was such a great experience. He is a man of profound wisdom.
A.P.J.: You guys did a good job. I particularly liked the way Kakarla Subbarao revered the human life:

"I am more concerned with human life than anything else in the whole Cosmos; to me how a man lives is more fascinating than how a star dies. If there is a God, He is present as much in the creation of each of us as He was at the creation of the Earth. The human condition is the mystery that engages my fascination, not society, country, humanity, and so on. To me, man is God, the centre of everything. Those who accomplish the most—measured in money, intelligence, skills, happiness, or love—are the ones who make the most of their genetic inheritance."[94]

A.T.: What do you find special in Kakarla Subbarao?

A.P.J.: His striking sincerity.

A.T.: Will you please elaborate?

A.P.J.: In the process of absolute sincerity, one can sometimes gain an insight into what is likely to occur. Kakarla Subbarao is like that. He says, "I cannot go to cure the body of my patient, but I can call out to God for his soul."

A.T.: I heard both of you talking about the prevailing uneasiness in our society. Will you share your thoughts?

A.P.J.: It was a very interesting discussion. Why good people heading Institutions are so uneasy? That was the issue. This happens when opportunity gives you the obligation to create. On one hand, you are content to meet the demands of the moment, work from one day to the next. On the other hand, you are anxious for others' approval and jealous of the possibility that they may become famous. You start wondering what will happen in the end to what you have done and been.

A.T.: Is it bad or undesirable to be uneasy?

A.P.J.: Not at all. On the contrary it is good. Bless your uneasiness as it is a sign that there is still life in you. Many people lie dormant and dead behind a facade of great ability, loyalty and ambition.

A.T.: And how do we define uneasiness?

A.P.J.: Two ideas: First, you are serving but you are not sure if that is enough, and second, you are doing something worthy but you are not sure of your worth. It is a sense of fear as to what posterity will say about you after you cease to be, or that may be it will say nothing.

A.T.: I never could gauge the depth and ferocity of your uneasiness.

A.P.J.: All of us don't know many things.

A.T.: How do you find Kakarla Subbarao a guiding soul?

A.P.J.: He is very human—a bundle of polarities. He is so competent and yet hesitant. He is so serene and yet so edgy. He is so virtuous and yet not a winner in the worldly sense. Kakarla Subbarao possesses that light which is Hidden God flickering in the turbulence of a human heart. This is his greatness and his tragedy, as well.

A.T.: 'Greatness and tragedy,' sound so paradoxical.

A.P.J.: Understanding paradoxes is essential. Most of the time, you are not able to live by the golden mean, but we must live without rest in the tension between mutually exclusive demands. This quality comes from age. My friend C.N.R. Rao[95] is a good example. Excellence is not an act for him, but a habit. He has motivated an entire generation of scientists and still works tirelessly.

A.T.: May I now tell how I see you as my guiding soul?

A.P.J.: Do you?

A.T.: Let me say so. You see things as they are. You can see through the beautiful appearance of things which are actually ugly. The ugly appearance of those things which are in reality beautiful does not deter you from dealing with them. You keep showing me each thing as it is and its true colour lest I fall into a snare and be ever errant.

A.P.J.: God bless you.

□

Part III

THE ESSENCE

O human race,
Our Lord is the Most Bounteous,
Who in silence speaks
Teaches what we know not.

Love is the mission of humanity
Be in the world like a traveller
And reckon yourself as of the dead
O human race.

A.T.: I can now see that essence is central to a human life. From Emperor Asoka to Verghese Kurien and Kakarla Subbarao, there is a clear manifestation of essence—something that was already there, embedded into the genes. The question is what leads the essence to manifest?

A.P.J.: I would like to slightly modify your statement. Instead of saying that essence is central to the human life, embedded in the genes; a better explanation would be that essence is central to the process of the journey of a human presence to liberation and development; the unique combination of genes produce unique capabilities and possibilities.

A.T.: Process and development are very unambiguous and straight-forward words. I am happy that I have finally landed onto some familiar ground. Please say more on liberation.

A.P.J.: By liberation, I mean dispelling the darkness of ignorance first and then, the fancies and notions that cloud the essence. The free man is not he who defies the rules. A free man is one who recognises the compulsions inherent in his being and seeks to read, learn, and inwardly digest each day's experience rather than be carried away by it.

A.T.: That is very clear. So, would you say that this is the purpose of a human life for which you are using the term 'presence'.

A.P.J.: A particular presence; a unique presence.

A.T.: How do we observe the performance of a human

life, the efficacy of this unique presence?

A.P.J.: The manner in which a presence evolves on this planet can be divided into three sub-processes: the awareness of the presence to the essence; the unique presence living with the essence; and the unique presence and essence combination becoming an eternal presence.

A.T.: Great. It is clear to me now. It's like a journey. More accurately, it is a composite journey involving three expeditions.

A.P.J.: Again words, but of course, appropriate and appealing.

A.T.: The first phase of the expedition is to be aware of the path. It takes a while for one to know about what his path in a life-time is.

A.P.J.: Different people come to realise it at different stages or phases of life. Some become aware of it quite early, like say, Ramanujan and Edison, some quite late, like Gandhiji and Caliph Umar. Sometimes, the purpose emerges in a very identifiable form as was the case with Edison and Verghese Kurien. For some, like Satish Dhawan and Kakarla Subbarao, the purpose remains essentially elusive.

A.T.: What happens once the path is known?

A.P.J.: Once the path is known, a lot of work goes into maintaining the orientation and developing inner capacities. This comes out of living in awareness and digesting experience vis-à-vis one's self. Lincoln and Nelson Mandela spent years on this journey.

A.T.: And where does this work eventually lead to?

A.P.J.: This effort culminates in the discovery of the presence of essence, and in learning to recognise it in its various forms and qualities. It commenced in C.V. Raman's life during his return voyage from England. It happened to Gandhiji when he was thrown out of the first class railway compartment in South Africa. Many years of development that followed marked their journey.

A.T.: I can clearly see your point. This is perhaps what Irish novelist James Joyce refers to as epiphany—a moment of sudden intuitive understanding, a flash of insight or an experience that occasions such a moment. This triggers the third journey—the unique combination of presence and essence becoming an eternal presence. By the same logic, what sets off the second journey—the unique presence living with the essence?

A.P.J.: The transition from the first to the second journey is not marked by a particular experience. There is a process of discovery involved though, whose central element is the initial experience and recognition of presence.

A.T.: How can we understand this better?

A.P.J.: This discovery happens in two phases. It starts with the awareness of our presence on this planet as essence in a body—an awareness dawns on us that we are indeed an inalienable part of humanity. We feel, we know, what humanity is. We become aware of its inner truth and potential. We may in fact feel connected with the rest of humanity, and we tend to identify ourselves with the whole of humanity.

A.T.: May I ask if you ever experienced it?

A.P.J.: Yes, I did experience it. In 1993, I was speaking to the DRDO Scientific Community and I posed a question, "Can my brain remove your pain?" This led to the creation of the Society for Biomedical Technology (SBMT) that has brought doctors and technologists together to develop indigenous medical devices and products. Why did I do that? I became aware of the new potential of what I was doing. Concern for the common man dawned on me, my consciousness could engage my essence. You were a part of SBMT.

A.T.: Not that I felt that way. You gave a call and I heeded to it amongst many other engineering professionals. B. Soma Raju was only one doctor who heard it. And thus came into being the legendary Kalam-Raju Stent. Similarly, B.N. Prasad led you to develop Floor Reaction Orthosis (FRO) for polio affected children from a missile composite material.

A.P.J.: You are good at structuring facts into impressive stories.

A.T.: What happens next? You said there are two phases.

A.P.J.: This engagement with essence is like getting on to a vessel—and sailing off to a voyage of inner exploration.

A.T.: Sailing off to a voyage of inner exploration on a vessel, it is such an enticing metahor. But how would you describe this phenomenon?

A.P.J.: In the inner journey, the consciousness goes through an elaborate process of clarification and purification—and the essence unfolds in its various aspects and dimensions. These newer forms of essence keep getting integrated with the presence.

A.T.: But the same thing happens when a child grows into an adult. The instinctual animal tendencies evolve into a civilised adult demeanour.

A.P.J.: There is a difference. The process of essential development takes one's inner self from its initial condition at the completion of ego-development, in which animal tendencies live camouflaged in a civilised veneer of ego-structures.

A.T.: You mean ego-development is not necessarily the development of the soul.

A.P.J.: It is not. The discovery and integration of essence transforms the soul from its condition of being primarily instinctually driven to the state of being primarily reason and compassion guided, with a heart. *Qalb*.

A.T.: Then what happens?

A.P.J.: What transforms instinctively driven conduct to compassion and reason guided action is its becoming receptive and transparent to the essence. When the essence manifests itself through the attitudes and actions of the soul, we recognize that the inner self now behaves on a more human plane, with lesser distortions of perception. *Taqliyya-i-sirr.*

A.T.: Is this the task of the second journey?

A.P.J.: This is primarily the task of the second journey of presence. While the first phase was journey to the essence, now this is journey with the essence. The presence journeys here in the company of essence, receptive to it and guided by it.

A.T.: Can you give me an example?

A.P.J.: Warrior Asoka spreads *Ahimsa Dharma*. Engineer Kurien gets into dairy development and goes on to create a great cooperative movement transforming the lives of millions. You work in a hospital.

A.T.: And what happens in the second journey?

A.P.J.: As the soul integrates the essence in its various qualities, it matures and develops its virtues, capacities, and faculties.

A.T.: Any example?

A.P.J.: Einstein is a good example. He always appeared to have a clear view of the problems of physics and the determination to solve them. He was able to visualise the main stages on the way to his goal. In fact, Einstein was forthright when he described his great achievements as mere stepping-stones from the previous to the next advance.

A.T.: So, essentially this is a process of maturation.

A.P.J.: Not maturation but integration. Once the essence

is touched, it functions as the crystallising point around which the soul integrates all its personal experiences of its potential arising in interaction with the events of everyday life.

A.T.: Where does ego fit in—'I' and 'mine'?
A.P.J.: The ego structure, which is nothing more than a fancy, a product of the mind, gives one the false sense of being an autonomous and unique individual. This structure is constructed through fixed mental impressions in the soul. The identity of the ego is the primary barrier. The ego structure confronts the soul with its inherent narcissism.

A.T.: Indeed, according to the legend of Narcissus, the Greek boy fell in love with his own reflection.
A.P.J.: The independence from narcissism is self-realisation. The essence begins to merge seamlessly with the presence. The duality of essence and presence begins to be bridged. Increasingly, the presence recognises the fact that it is nothing but the simplicity and exquisiteness of timeless essence. Caliph Umar's and Gandhiji's lives are perfect examples of this process.

A.T.: And what about your life?
A.P.J.: You are a funny fellow.

A.T.: How exactly does it happen? Is it a gradual process or a sudden phenomenon?
A.P.J.: The realisation of the essence is mostly a developmental process. However, the mission of a human life is mostly discovered.

A.T.: In terms of behavioural parameters, how does it happen?

A.P.J.: Once the essence is found and gets activated, one's actions turn more intelligent, compassionate, clear, steadfast and fuller. The actions can be physical, expressive or mental. Umar's purity and righteousness, Subbulakshmi's music and Ramanujan's mathematics are representative examples.

A.T.: I can visualise the process now. You quit a Cabinet rank position and went to Anna University and became a teacher.

A.P.J.: You are leading me somewhere.

A.T.: That's how I see it. You were explaining the symbiotic presence-essence relationship?

A.P.J.: Once activated, the essence turns into a dynamic living presence and its morphogenic transformations express the pure perfections of true nature, indeed a symbiotic relationship of great value.

A.T.: Is true nature inherited?

A.P.J.: No. True nature is the latent human potential. It is like the sheepness of a sheep or the dogness of a dog.[96]

A.T.: Then what happens to the essence while this potential is unfolding?

A.P.J.: During the unfolding of the human potential, or in other words, during the manifestation of the essence, the soul progresses from the stage of essence to the stage of a part of the essence becoming an angelic soul, a guiding soul.

A.T.: Sometime back you spoke about the animal tendencies.

A.P.J.: Not many possibilities exist for the unfolding of human potential during the annihilation of animal tendencies. Nevertheless this process leads to finding the essence and to the recognition of the dynamic field and medium of the soul.

A.T.: I think I am undergoing that.

A.P.J.: No. The essence of a writer has already begun to find expression in your effort.

A.T.: Thank you for your very kind words.

A.P.J.: The essence asserts itself in various aspects. In your case, the most apparent aspect is writing. But other aspects are bound to be there, interwoven, interrelated.

A.T.: Such as?

A.P.J.: Imagination, sensitivity and the ability to construct thoughts and mould expressions, for example.

A.T.: What is the decisive factor or force of such a phenomenon in life? At what juncture does it happen?

A.P.J.: Past experiences and its repression are the toughest barriers. We are all conditioned by the impressions from the past. This conditioning mostly remains outside of consciousness and functions automatically. The moment one liberates himself from this conditioning, the essence gets activated.

A.T.: I used to think of this conditioning and repression as something good. An individual manages to evolve in spite of intolerable difficulties by trying not be aware of them through various methods of repression.

A.P.J.: There is hardly anything good in this. The repressed material does not disappear but remains hidden in what psychology terms the unconscious, exerting a powerful force on conscious experience. This gets reflected in people's habits, addictions, moods, blunders and reckless impulses.

A.T.: One of the momentous discoveries of modern psychology is that the conditioning of early years can be released by retracting conflict and painful manifestations and symptoms to their unconscious roots. In *First and Last Freedom*, Jiddu Krishnamurti termed it as strife, battle, the conflict of becoming.[97]

A.P.J.: You work with psychologists in your hospital. What do they say about it?

A.T.: I once asked my psychologist friend, B. Anand, to give me an everyday life example of the essential dynamics of the mind's functioning. He gave me the example of issues related with strength. He told me that difficulty with anger and aggression, as a stance of passivity and weakness, is indeed an unresolved strength issue.

A.P.J.: How?

A.T.: A child who must be passive and submissive before a parent, need not repeat this pattern once he or she is a grown-up adult. Exploring the energy of this emotion can reveal its connection to strength. Anger is indeed a distortion of innate emotional strength.[98]

A.P.J.: You mean the quality of strength becomes caught up in the emotion of anger.

A.T.: Yes Sir. The soul is afraid to own up her strength because of the fear of invoking the anger of one's parents. So, it abandons and represses its strength causing the distorted emotion of anger. Working through this issue opens up the quality of strength in the soul.

A.P.J.: It is so very fascinating. What does your psychologist friends say about the other emotional problems human beings face?

A.T.: They use the term "Existential issues" to describe problems related to the normal limitations of being a human being living in a world with others. These issues include questions, conflicts, and suffering in relation to desire and desirelessness, gratification and frustration, intimacy and isolation, relatedness and aloneness, love and aggression, instinct and reason, limitation and finitude, transitoriness and mortality, choice and accident, meaning and emptiness, being and nothingness, fear and dread, and so on.

A.P.J.: Don't tell me your doctor friends use all these story bound words.

A.T.: Well, they explain the existential issues in dreadful clinical terms. There is so much good general literature available on this matter. I picked up these words from there.

A.P.J.: Whatever each one of us possesses is all picked up material. You picked up some very appealing words.

A.T.: The main existential issue is that the soul lives an embodied life with its normal limitations and frustrations. These are further compounded by its ignorance of its true nature.

A.P.J.: I think it is very important to have a mind that is open to everything, and attached to nothing. Go ahead with existential issues.

A.T.: Existential issues tend to arise naturally in life, especially during transitions and intense events. They can however, be brought forth through inner work. They arise especially as the soul learns to penetrate and transcend its ego structure. Franz Kafka[99] wrote his celebrated masterpiece *Metamorphosis* on this theme.

A.P.J.: I can see that. The period that followed the failure of the first flight of SLV-3 and the pre-launch difficulties in Agni's first flight trial made me discover my real self in a very significant manner. But the Arakonam crash in 1999, was a devastating experience for me, also in terms of what it did to my ego-structure.

A.T.: You have never discussed that. I could only see the tip of the iceberg of the enormous pain that you have always kept submerged in the ocean of your work. Would you like to share it?

A.P.J.: More than the sharing aspect, I wish to express my gratitude to the eight young men who sacrificed their lives in a scientific endeavour. The nation must know about those unsung heroes. The pain their family suffered must be shared.

A.T.: Sir, are you talking about the Airborne Surveillance Platform (ASP) crash on 11 January, 1999?

A.P.J.: Yes. The ASP crashed into the dense forests near Arakonam.

A.T.: I spoke once with K. Ramchand[100] about this incident. He was the system engineer. He told me that the Avro aircraft, with airborne surveillance system mounted atop as a motodome[101], took off around 1400 hrs, climbed up to 10,000 ft and set course toward the Chennai coast. The radar testing was carried out between the Arakonam-Chennai coastline. The target aircraft for the mission trial was an AN-32 aircraft, which took off 15 minutes before the Avro. The radar performance was checked with both sea and land clutter. The performance of the radar as reported by the onboard mission crew via very high frequency communication was very good. After 1½ hours of flight testing, the target aircraft landed at Arakonam around 1600 hrs. Subsequently, the ASP aircraft set course from Chennai towards Arakonam and descended close to the airfield from 10,000 ft to 5,000 ft. When the aircraft was about 5 nautical miles away from the airfield at an altitude between 3,000 ft and 5,000 ft, the motodome severed away from the aircraft. The aircraft became unstable and crashed immediately at about 1620 hrs killing all the eight occupants.

A.P.J.: I was in a Defence Research Council Meeting in my office in the South Block when I was told about the crash. I rushed to Bangalore to be with the bereaved families. Air Chief Marshal A.Y. Tipnis was also there. It was a very difficult moment for me, seeing the young wives crying in desperation and parents standing shell-shocked. One lady thrust her infant into my lap, saying—"Who will look after this young life?" Another lady cried, "Why did you do this to us Mr. Kalam?"

A.T.: Ramchand gave me the list of the officers who lost their lives. Sqn Ldr P. Venkataraman was piloting the aircraft. P. Ilango, instrumentation engineer, and K.P. Shaju, radar system engineer, were from the Centre for Airborne Systems (CABS); D. Narasimhaswamy, Radar processing scientist, and I. Jayakumar, Signal processing Scientist, were from Electronics Research and Development Establishment (LRDE); and Sqn Ldrs N.V. Seshu, R. Bhatnagar and S. Ravi were the other Air Force officers.

A.P.J.: There were hardly any remains. For the comfort of the families, authorities made coffins and kept them in the community hall.

A.T.: O my God!

A.P.J.: In my state of profound grief, I could barely mumble a few words in the farewell speech I had to make. Later in the night I wrote:

The lamps are different
But the light is same.
Worldly joys you returned to the world
You remain in my innermost soul.

A.T.: It reminds me of the letter Abraham Lincoln wrote to a mother of five sons[102] who had died gloriously in the civil war.

"I feel how weak and fruitless must be any words of mine which should attempt to beguile you from the grief of a loss so overwhelming. But I cannot refrain from tendering to you the consolation that may be found in the thanks of the Republic they died to save.

I pray that our Heavenly Father may assuage the anguish of your bereavement, and leave you only the cherished memory of the loved and lost, and the solemn pride that must be yours, to have laid so costly a sacrifice upon the altar of freedom."

A.P.J.: The memory of wailing widows, immobilized parents, an innocent infant in my lap and the cremation of symbolic coffins haunts me sitting here in Rashtrapati Bhavan. Do the few around going through the motions of politics and protocol understand the pain and agony people suffer out there in the laboratories and fields?

A.T.: What is the message?

A.P.J.: Don't pretend to be a candle, be a moth. Know the power hidden in serving. We seem to have got stuck with external forms of politics and mistaking them to be nation-building. It is sacrifices, toil and valour that is seldom shown or seen that truly makes a nation.

A.T.: I understand that you had a lot of difficulty in arranging relief of about Rs. 700,000 for each family?

A.P.J.: I have forgotten that. There is a point, at which everything becomes simple and there is no longer any question of choice, because all you have staked will be lost if you look back. Life, all through, is marked by points of no return—that is where I stood at that time.

A.T.: First time, I see in you manifestation of pain.

A.P.J.: I am sad. Are we failing our people?

A.T.: You said something similar in the Parliament recently (March 2005).

A.P.J.: Well what I said was that the arithmetical compulsions of incremental numbers and alleged tradability of certain legislative seats, won perhaps through means allegedly dubious and undemocratic, makes me feel uneasy. When politics degrades itself to political adventurism, the nation would be on the calamitous road to inevitable disaster and ruination. Let us not risk that.

A.T.: You must have experienced loneliness.

A.P.J.: Yes. A profound sense of aloneness indeed. In sadness, one has to be alone. But as things got sorted out around me and I discovered the intrinsic intimacy of essential presence, I realised that my essence constitutes a much more fundamental connectedness than that was known by my ego-self.

A.T.: So, there is a trade-off. Even though the inner journey confronts us, often painfully, with existential issues, the experience and understanding of essence provides resolution and a depth of wisdom.

A.P.J.: I would call it a phase when the soul goes beyond the mind.

A.T.: *Going beyond the mind* is a beautiful phrase. Will you elaborate on this experience?

A.P.J.: The habit of turning fear immediately into thought and action, leads to a defensive trap that snags our humanity. The mind wants us to fear the unknown, the unfamiliar. It does this by creating a division between 'what is' and what it wants us to think things 'should be'. This dissonance keeps the mind in an overactive, continually problem solving state of consciousness.

A.T.: I can understand now some of my own reactions.

A.P.J.: The solutions that present themselves in this state of mind, lead to a vicious cycle of more repetitive thoughts and actions. These actions may temporarily relieve the body, but they leave the mind prone to search other means of future escape. This increases the drive for more activity and offers no real solutions.

A.T.: Indeed, endless, purposeless activity eventually leads to helpless feelings that perpetuate another cycle of more meaningless thoughts and actions.

A.P.J.: When you observe all experience in a beyond mind state, ignoring escape tactics of the mind through thought and action, the relaxed and quieted consciousness opens to spirit-guided messages.

A.T.: Will you elaborate on these messages? What kind of messages?

A.P.J.: These messages function like encrypted computer programs that, when their encryption is deciphered, unfold according to a specific content and logic.

A.T.: Where do they come from?

A.P.J.: They rise from the deepest and most fundamental truths of its nature and grounded in the continuity of genetic stock.

A.T.: I have two questions. First, what is the nature of essence? What are its characteristics? Second, how do we experience essence?

A.P.J.: You are missing the fundamentals here. It is questionable to think of essence as having characteristics, for it is completely indeterminable. It possesses no explicit qualities, no recognizable differentiations.

A.T.: A major insight of developmental psychology is that the sense that "I am an autonomous individual" is based on the ego structure of boundaries; at this point the soul may begin to recognize this fact in painful and intimate personal experience. The ego takes us on a never-ending 'now reject-now hope-now desire' cycle of experience.

A.P.J.: Will you elaborate on the "autonomous individual" concept?

A.T.: Sir, this term comes originally from Rousseau[103]. It is in vogue amongst postmodernists. An autonomous individual literally means someone choosing his own values and identity. To be an autonomous individual meant to choose a way of life or conception of the good that conformed to the Universal principles of pure practical reason and therefore to take one's direction and bearings not from government, religion, habit, or appetite, but rather from laws deriving from principles inherent in one's innermost metaphysically real self.

A.P.J.: I believe that goodness is a fundamental characteristic of essence. It is a timeless potential that might reveal itself at any point or any place. It is unblemished goodness, incorruptible goodness, indestructible goodness. It is divine. It is not parcelled out to individuals. It is totally boundless, unlimited and endless. I like your sons' names—Aseem and Amol—both symbolise this boundlessness.

A.T.: Does it mean that everyone is essentially good?

A.P.J.: My answer is yes. The world operates on spiritual principles just as it operates on the laws of physics and gravity. It is up to us to learn what these principles are and then to choose to live by them.

A.T.: This thought gives such a good feeling.

A.P.J.: There is goodness in the world—not in the discrete and reified forms[104] of the world, not some attraction vying for your attention—but in the depth of the world, in its ultimate nature. It's not shaped by current opinion or whim. It is not determined by people. Goodness is impartial because it applies equally to everyone throughout the world—what is 'real' good for me must be good to every one else on this planet. The law of Goodness, if I may call it so, is self-enforcing and is not dependent on human authority or commandments.

A.T.: How does one follow it?

A.P.J.: You can so easily see this by baring your soul of its obscuration, and surrender it completely to this perception. By surrendering the illusion of a separate self and its own *will*, the soul will find this goodness. If the soul lets itself truly fall, all the way, not into the hands of one person or another, one form or another, but absolutely and fully to the Will of God—*Insha Allah*—it will be received with grace and love—unfailingly.

A.T.: You mentioned *qalb*, the psychological or emotional heart. Is this the psychological space where goodness dwells?

A.P.J.: Let me use a metaphor for a change. There is a need for mirrors in a house and the need for televisons in the country to help mankind see things. Likewise in man's body, the psychological heart, like a special mirror, can possibly serve man in better determining the nature and the methods of utilization of all things.

Just as a mirror does not discriminate between ugliness and beauty, *qalb* sees good everywhere and in everybody. It insists that all is good and by refusing to see anything but good, it tends to cause that quality to appear in itself and in other things.

A.T.: Why do we then suffer?
A.P.J.: When the divine light in *qalb* is dimmed, like the dust covers a mirror, the original effects get muted, become blocked and distorted. Many feelings and emotions that characterise human experience now mushroom. We now have frustration, barrenness, anger, rage, hatred, sadness, pain, fear, deprivation, loss, jealousy, envy, pride, and the many other well-known difficult emotions of the human heart.

A.T.: Sir, I always found you at ease even in difficult situations. You have been so caring and yet so unruffled in the face of adversity, even casual.
A.P.J.: Give me an example.

A.T.: When Haridwar Singh, our colleague in DRDO, was declared seriously ill on account of his liver dysfunction, it was a very difficult situation. He had a very valuable life and scientific career ahead, a lot to contribute. Liver transplant was the only possibility left to save his life. But Government rules, even a Supreme Court ruling, would not allow his treatment abroad. I recall, this was in 1998.
A.P.J.: You are right. And even the expenses involved were huge. A liver transplant in England would cost about Rs. 60-80 lakhs.[105] But I was so sure of what I was doing—operating on an impossible mission without doubt.

A.T.: I met Haridwar Singh and his wife on the eve of their departure to London. He was looking very pale—a mere skeleton, barely able to sit.

A.P.J.: He later told me about the big pep talk you gave him. You shared with him your earlier visit to King's Hospital in London and explained quite positively to him the possibility of his revival with intense certainty.

A.T.: Yes Sir. I had been to King's Hospital earlier and indeed brought back with me the dream of an Indian liver transplant facility.

A.P.J.: Well, this eventually became a reality at multiple centres and today no one needs to go abroad for a liver transplant.

A.T.: Isn't this a real-life illustration of what you once said—"dreams lead to thoughts; thoughts lead to action; actions transform life?"

A.P.J.: You manage to infect the people around you with your enthusiasm.

A.T.: I met Haridwar Singh recently. Seven years down the line, with a British liver in his system, he was in the pink of health, back from a teaching assignment abroad on Nanotechnology.

A.P.J.: Once you operate on your essence, which is made of the purest and gentlest love, it impacts the soul in ways it had always longed for, but could not fully attain. Its softness is soothing, lulling the mind into rest, the body into natural relaxation, and heart into serene openness. Something of this kind happened with Haridwar Singh. I am happy.

A.T.: I would say that once you are touched by a heavenly soothing hand, you spontaneously feel at ease, letting go like a baby responding to its loving mother's intimate holding and comforting.

A.P.J.: Absolutely!

A.T.: And I would say that under the command of essence, the body melts, as if it had been on a prolonged vacation in Andamans, leaving all worry in Chennai.

A.P.J.: How do you create so many fantastic scenes?

A.T.: This mental wandering, this peripatetic interaction, should I say, helps me understand better. Coming back to our discussion, *qalb* is the battleground of two warring armies: those of *nafs*, or worldly nature, and *ruh,* or spirit.

A.P.J.: Why don't you say it is a transmitter and receiver from person to person and from servant to Glorious God.

A.T.: You are using excellent metaphors.

A.P.J.: The soothing and graceful characteristics and features of essence indeed challenge beliefs and positions strongly held by the *nafs*, instituted in its structure and identity. *Nafs* tells us to believe that the world is basically unsafe, or at best neutral. This attitude of basic distrust impels one to continually resort to strategies and devices to protect and defend his personal ground.

A.T.: I can see this well. Autonomy brings a strong defensive attitude. You feel that you need to take things into your own hands, that unless you take precautions and make arrangements, your interests will not be automatically taken care of. I have seen many powerful people living always on alert, even paranoid, so sure and certain that things will not go as they should; that the moment their guard is lowered, their lives will fall apart.

A.P.J.: An attitude of basic trust is necessary not only for the ease and security of the soul, but also for it to be connected to its essence, which is how it can unfold and develop. Prophet Joseph (*Hazrat Yusuf*

Alaih Assalaam) himself testified to God's blessings on him:

> "God has been indeed gracious to us. Whoever acts in fear of God and full submission to Him and is patient, surely God does not waste the reward of those who are perfectly good."[106]

A.T.: I can say from personal experience that the discovery and integration of divine love gives one great support and momentum in terms of one's growth. After I recovered from a cardiac arrest, the whole Universe seemed to have gathered and presented all that was needed—medical expertise, nursing care, all the required financial and emotional support. During the 49 days I had to spend in the hospital, not a day passed when I did not receive flowers and books. Even you came.

A.P.J.: You are blessed. The more deeply the soul gets

integrated with divine love, the more completely it evolves in terms of wisdom. As a result, the more trusting will it be that its unfoldment will proceed guided and held, that its needs on the journey will be met and difficulties resolved. This trust was given to me by my parents.

A.T.: I can never forget the trust you gave me at least on three occasions—integrate my pain—twice it was pain of the body, experienced on the physical plane and once it was higher pain, pain of life, if I may say so. I feel indeed protected and secure.

A.P.J.: This security indeed emancipates you from the routine of ordinary activity and inspires you to seek more in life, particularly to pursue sublime values related to love, truth and reality. When I voluntarily left the position of Principal Scientific Advisor to the Government of India and took up teaching at Anna University, I did precisely that.

A.T.: And then you became the President of India.

A.P.J.: I learnt that the *unfoldment* of my soul was supported by the real Universe itself, that it was not in my own hands, and that it was infinitely better that it was in the hands of loving divinity. Such basic trust and unfoldment of the soul spurs you on the journey forward, accelerating the unfoldment of the soul and the revelation of essence and its wisdom.

A.T.: You have acknowledged the guidance you received from some of the great guiding souls who walked on this planet. They were all remarkably accomplished.

How did these accomplishments come from the fusion of the presence into a formless absolute of essence?

A.P.J.: There you are; you've hit the bull's eye now. All the souls I mentioned here in this book achieved self-realisation of the absolute essence. But that was not what marked their journey on this planet. How would we have known but for something that happened beyond this?

A.T.: Do you mean their accomplishments in the physical world?

A.P.J.: I would like to describe it as the essence unfolding.

36 A.T.: Having reached the plane of absolute essence, transcending the physical and the mundane, how do we then return? Is there something like descent after the ascent?

A.P.J.: I think you have used very precise words, though unknowingly and perhaps, quite unconsciously. The inner journey of the presence to the essence has been a journey of ascent, of moving from the lowest and grossest dimensions of experience to the summit of subtlety and truth. As our aspiration is, so is our inspiration. The higher nature takes our fragmentary knowledge, thought, experience, and our aspiration, which is sacrifice, and it is transfigured, made whole and returned to us.

A.T.: Will you please elaborate?

A.P.J.: Gandhiji is a perfect example of this journey. He perceived the purest spiritual nature within and throughout the grossest of his country.

A.T.: How do we see it in terms of ascent and descent?

A.P.J.: In this upward journey, the process is primarily that of discrimination, separation, purification, and resolution. Its nature reveals itself as simpler, more subtle, and increasingly devoid of forms, qualities, determinations and concepts. Gandhiji moved toward absolute simplicity, through a process of continual shedding. All forms and dimensions were shed to reveal the perfect simplicity and emptiness of the absolute essence.

A.T.: And what is the journey of descent?

A.P.J.: The journey of descent is backward movement from the vantage point of the absolute through the same dimensions of manifestation. In the process of descent, Gandhiji learned that there is no leaving the essence, but that descent is simply the integration of all dimensions of manifestation into the absolute. Chauri Chaura[107] is one example. Noakhali is another.

A.T.: Gandhiji was shaken by the violence of Chauri Chaura and abruptly called off the non-cooperation movement in 1922, when the movement was at its peak. Chauri Chaura, he said, was a 'divine warning' that the masses were not yet prepared for launching the right kind of struggle to gain freedom for the country.

A.P.J.: I saw a letter written by Phillips Talbot, South Asia correspondent of the *Chicago Daily*. He travelled to Noakhali and spent time with Mahatma Gandhi during the communal violence there preceding Independence. The letter is dated 16 February, 1947. He wrote:

"It was revealing to watch Gandhi throwing himself during this critical season into the remoteness of East Bengal's Noakhali district for a barefooted village-to-village pilgrimage in search of Hindu-Muslim amity. Here was a 77-year-old ascetic, rising above the physical ordeal, immersed in a peculiarly Indian approach to the cleavage that threatens the country.

I walked with him for half an hour in the sweeper's settlement where he stayed and talked of the wave of mass fratricide which was then rolling over the country. Although he denied letting emotions affect his judgement, we sensed a feeling of frustration, if not of failure. This had nothing to do with the validity of the creed of non-violence itself. Its truth, he repeated, could never be challenged. But he could not be happy with the way in which his teachings were being flouted."[108]

A.T.: May I offer a metaphor?

A.P.J.: This book is getting quite figurative.

A.T.: In the journey upwards, the individual soul penetrates the various dimensions of creation, which are garments beneath which the essence was unseen. The journey of descent is taking off these garments revealing essence and then moving with the dressed up essence in the same garments that were earlier hiding it.

A.P.J.: The journey of ascent is that of shedding and separation leading to the simplicity of singleness, the journey of descent is that of integration and union leading to the richness of wholeness.

A.T.: And what is the outcome of this integration?
A.P.J.: Creation.

A.T.: O my God! This is a far-reaching idea. Ordinarily we perceive a world of objects. So many different objects populating the space. These objects are in a state of constant change; there is a linear progression from the past to the future.
A.P.J.: The normal perception of movement and change in objects, this linear progression from the past to the future, is an outcome of a particular point of view.

A.T.: Sir, another analogy comes to my mind.
A.P.J.: Go ahead.

A.T.: There is a cinema screen. We see a man moving across the screen, but in fact there is no movement. The totality of the picture changes from one frame to the next. Because this change of frames happens gradually, and because the changes occur faster than our eyes can discern, we see a continuous picture of a man walking.
A.P.J.: You are right. Each point on the screen is going through a transformation. The total effect of a man walking across the screen is indeed a sequence of different frames. The walking man is actually a part of the whole picture, and the whole picture changes. In reality, there is no man, just a picture changing its details.

A.T.: It is scary. Going by this concept, meeting you, working on this book, this exchange of ideas, all this has nothing to do with you and me.

A.P.J.: Who are we anyway? Our Essence is just unfolding. The words we are exchanging now, you will present as text tomorrow and the publisher will bring out a book the next day. Someone, somewhere, will read it. Something written in the book will trigger something in the reader, and will possibly lead to a change in his situation, surroundings. It happened when our book *Wings of Fire* reached millions. Where are you in that, where am I?

A.T.: Sir, I think I am baffled. Does it mean that no man has walked on the face of the Earth? No human has ever taken one step? No one was ever born or has lived? It is all the appearance and outer forms of essence that changes, and what we term movement is the appearance of changes of some locations?

A.P.J.: Look at this very present moment. You are talking to me now in Rashtrapati Bhavan. It is such a great building! There is so much grandeur, so much beauty around us. People come here, receive awards. There are so many ceremonies. Visitors who come here feel great, excited, elated. At the same time, there are employees, guards, house-keepers, gardeners, and so on, who are posted here. For them it is part of their job. Where I am sitting now, Lord Irwin was sitting in 1931. Sarvepalli Radhakrishnan sat on this chair. Where was I then? Where are they now? Tomorrow someone else will sit here. The reality is in here and now. It was real when it was. It is real when it is. It will be real when it will be.

A.T.: Is not the reality of the moment A.P.J. Abdul Kalam talking to Arun Tiwari?

A.P.J.: That is an illusion, including A.P.J. Abdul Kalam and Arun Tiwari. The reality is the exchange of our ideas at this moment. The unfolding of essence through us—you and I, is the reality.

A.T.: I feel I am getting to the Truth.

A.P.J.: The Truth is nothing but dispelling an illusion. In our comfortable houses and work places, the terrible suffering of the villages and urban slums seem distant, abstract and unreal and we can somehow imagine that it hasn't anything to do with us.

A.T.: It reminds me of a poem by Geoffrey Hill wherein he laments the absence of a moral imagination:[109]

> "Evil is not goods's absence but gravity's
> everlasting bedrock and its fatal chains
> inert, violent, the suffrage of our days."

A.P.J.: There is constant process of creation-destruction through which each object exists. After this interaction, each of us will be different, our individual consciousness expanded, ignorance dispelled. All of existence is continually coming into being, where it is always a new existence. When I go to different places, talk to children; answer their questions, what is happening?

A.T.: Young minds get ignited.

A.P.J.: That is the point. A new India is getting unfolded. The reality is not that the President of India travelled to a village and met children in a school there. The reality is that such an interaction triggered something in some souls, some buds blossomed, and some caterpillars turned butterflies.

A.T.: The Universe is never old; it is always new, for it gets renewed instant to instant. This includes absolutely everything. It includes both animate and inanimate objects, the Earth and the Sky, the planets, the Sun and the stars, the galaxies and the space that contains them.

A.P.J.: It also includes all the thoughts, images, memories, feelings, sensations, and all phenomena, at all levels of being.

A.T.: And all this constitutes a dynamic entity, continuous and continuously coming into being.

A.P.J.: We can experience this directly when we become aware of the dimension of dynamic being. We do not simply perceive objects in space that move in time, but we experience ourselves as an infinite and boundless presence that continuously transforms itself into the various objects and forms of the Universe.

A.T.: Is that the reason why you chose to talk about Guiding Souls?

A.P.J.: Yes. The message I want to convey is that essence is the ground and nature of all forms. It is the substance that is in a process of constant transformation, and through this transformation, objects continue to appear and cease, after a point.

A.T.: One has to capture the essence.

A.P.J.: Exactly.

A.T.: Does it come from religious scholarship?

A.P.J.: There is great diversity in approaches to religious practice in regard to the relationship between belief, ritual and ethics. The contrast between Judaism and Christianity is a good example, with Islam positioning somewhere in between. Then there are Eastern religions.

A.T.: How do we go about then?

A.P.J.: Salvation is primary in some religions; others are more concerned with enlightenment. While Western approaches lay stress on soul and spirit, Eastern approaches are more concerned with mind and thought.

A.T.: What is the challenge?

A.P.J.: The challenge is to live a deliberate, studied, self-disciplined life, always considerate of others, always concerned for the common good; a life grounded in various habits that form a strong character.

A.T.: How do different religions fit in?

A.P.J.: What is this fitting business? My friend Y.S. Rajan gave me some of my best insights on Islamic tenets. Poetess Jyothirllata Girija wrote so beautifully *Pearls from the Prophet*.

A.T.: But there are differences. There are conflicts.

A.P.J.: There is lot of politics entered into religion. In fact, there are more divisions within religions than between them.

A.T.: These differences indeed depend upon the extent to which modernity and secularism are accommodated or excluded from the religious framework.

A.P.J.: You are right.

A.T.: Does religion stand as a challenge to modern values or does it adapt to them?

A.P.J.: Religion cannot be aloof and separate from modern society. The modernity must be engaged. Will religion succeed in changing worldly values in a more spiritual direction or will it be observed into the new set of values, transforming into something utterly different, something unrecognisable to its ancestors? That is the challenge.

A.T.: Sublime truths reveal themselves across boundaries of religion.

A.P.J. God loves those who are firm and steadfast. There have been individuals who bore patiently whatever befell them and carried on with their mission—whatever it was—faith, empire, mathematics, music and so on.

A.T.: So you say that essence generates forms and perceives them. It is the creator, the created, and the process of creation.

A.P.J.: I say that creation is simply generation, a continuous unfolding of forms and experiences. When we realise that there is ultimately no separate and autonomous soul, we see that there is no such thing as independent action, personal choice or volition. Everything is the expression of the Will of God. What we call action, doing, behaviour, and functioning are actually imaginary things. In reality there are no such things. The same one being is moving my hand and circling the Moon around the Earth.

A.T.: Where is then the space for free will that a human mortal enjoys?

A.P.J.: Free will is the engine that moves the soul on the right path.

A.T.: But it can cause it to stray from the right path also, don't you think so?

A.P.J.: The power of free will is that it will surely take you somewhere.

A.T.: May I ask you a personal question at the end?

A.P.J.: Go ahead.

A.T.: How would you describe your own inner journey?

A.P.J.: My inner journey is many things. It is a journey of adventure and discovery—from Rameswaram Island to Rashtrapati Bhavan—I covered a very long distance. It is a journey of maturation and completeness—from physics to aeronautics to satellite launch vehicles to guided missiles to nuclear weapons to management of human affairs, inquiring into faiths, unity of minds:

The domain kept expanding. It has been a journey of truth and authenticity; a journey of love, devotion, and passion; a journey of compassion, giving and service. It has been a journey of realisation of the nature of soul and reality; a journey of insight and learning; a journey of fulfilment of life and human potential; a journey of inner freedom. Journey, journey, journey...till the end.

A.T.: Do you feel there is something that has not yet happened, ground not yet covered?

A.P.J.: My journey of liberation from suffering and limitation is inconclusive. There is agony, uneasiness. People in villages are suffering avoidable hardships. Urban slums are full of adversities amidst the affluence of our development. There is violence, hatred amongst my people.

A.T.: You are hopeful of peace and harmony?

A.P.J.: Where is the doubt? My people will eventually get connected to their Indian essence which is grace, dignity, and compassion. Such connection will help them sail through the vicissitudes of life and the adversities of their times. Finally, they will live any life that fits their circumstances in harmony and peace.

A.T.: Why is peace still eluding our land? I want your parting thoughts on this.

A.P.J.: Read the following lines of Jalaluddin Rumi:

> "The angel is free because of his knowledge,
> The beast because of his ignorance.

Between the two remains the son of man to struggle."[110]

When you rule your mind, you rule your world. The Sun became the most powerful source of resplendent light only when it got hold of itself, so to say. Plants only began providing food when they achieved the discipline of evolving into crops. We have angels and we have beasts and one billion sons of man—struggling but insolent. When these people start respecting their existence, refusing to be defeated by their poverty, India will excel.

A.T.: God willing, let it be so.

□

NOTES

1. Paraphrased from Vietnamese Buddhist Monk Thich Nhat Hanh.
2. Adapted from 13th Century Turkish Poet Jalal-al-Din Muhammad Rumi.
3. The hut is in the Banyan Grove at Rashtrapati Bhavan.
4. Al-Ahzab; The Confederates; The Holy Quran 33.72.
5. Ashtavakra Gita consists dialogue between Sage Ashtavakra and King Janaka. Ashtavakra Gita is melody of interior brain, beyond the thought and feeling, which understands and always, remains drowned in the calmness.
6. Chapter 1, Stage 3.
7. Chapter 2, Text 25.
8. Subhash Kak teaches Electrical and Computer Engineering at the Louisiana State University.
9. Audio book based on *Wings of Fire.*
10. "Only you must be honest with yourselves.": *General Epistle of James (I, 22).*
11. Quoted in: Helminski, Kabir (2000). *The Rumi Collection.* P.19.
12. Unity of humanity.
13. Stage 1,19.
14. Ramana Maharishi (1879-1950) may be taken as the greatest devotee of formless *brahman.*
15. Friedrich Nietzsche (1844-1900) inquired into the foundations of traditional morality.
16. Jain seer and the head of the Terapanth school, A man striving for Universal Peace and Amity.

17. Originator of the Diamond Approach to Self-Realization and founder of The Ridhwan School.
18. American poet Walt Whitman (1819-1892) wrote, "One must let the true self out, just like the spider lets out his filament."
19. Meng Tzu, in Latinized form, Mencius (372-289 BC), based his thought on the concept of *jen* (humanness).
20. The thousand yard Model of the Solar System by Guy Ottewell (1989).
21. You are drunk, and this is the edge of the roof—Rumi.
22. Proverbs 29:18.
23. *Yad gatva na nivartante.* (Chapter 15, Text 6, Line 3).
24. Roman Emperor (161-180 AD).
25. "God hath given them the spirit of slumber, eyes that they should not see, and ears that they should not hear, unto this day" (Romans 11:8).
26. Rumi frequently used dung and musk as metaphors for profane and sublime. "No one discerns the musk from the dung. The town has become packed with dung worshippers."
27. The Analects, Book III (*Pa Yih),* Chapter XIII.
28. Jaya Row is founder of Vedanta Vision and teacher of Indian philosophy.
29. Vivekacudamani is one of the most important texts in the Advaita tradition and the most popular philosophical work ascribed to the great Indian philosopher, Sankara (650-700 AD).
30. The *Manu Smriti* were a code of conduct adopted by Aryan tribes, who first settled and later gradually expanded their dominance in the Indian subcontinent.
31. *Shangri-La,* or *Shambhala* in Tibetan, means the "sun and the moon in one's heart."
32. Ivan Rilski, was Bulgarian monk lived in ninth century. Under the 500-year rule of Ottoman Turks, he became a source of Bulgarian identity and culture.

33. Founder of the Franciscan Order lived during 1181-1226 AD in Italy.
34. Powell is widely recognized as one of the most inspired writers on the subject of *Advaita* the teaching of non-duality. "*True religion or spirituality is nothing other than the reversal of this whole process of chaos, conflict, to a state of simplicity, naturalness, and therefore order...*"
35. American Author lived during (1883-1970) is widely recognized as the founder of the modern genre of personal success literature.
36. Term 'Circle of Influence' is first used by author Steven Covey. "You also have to create time to get out of your comfort zone."
37. The complex connotations of this concepts is seen in Buddhist Tradition as Bardo. We can understand it as transcendental insight that may arise with the direct experience of reality.
38. Hazrat Inayat Khan (1882-1927) started 'The sufi Order in the West' (now called the Sufi Order International) in the early part of the 20th century.
39. A British writer lived during 1864-1912, James Allen teaches two essential truths: today we are where our thoughts have taken us, and we are the architects – for better or worse – of our futures.
40. Second President of India (1962-1967) lived during 1888-1975.
41. Carl Jung (1875-1961) was a Swiss psychiatrist who propagated the concepts of collective consciousness and synchronicity as an explanation for anything in the real world.
42. Mathnawi I, 3703-3706, quoted in: Helminsky, Kabir (2000). The Rumi collection. P.21.
43. Pythagoras (582-500 BC) is regarded as one of the brightest figures of early Greek antiquity.

44. Mathnawi IV:2348-2353, Version of Camille and Kabir Helminski "Rumi: Jewels of Remembrance" Threshold Books, 1996.
45. 321-185 BC, founded by Chandragupta Maurya (321-297 BC).
46. Kural 211.
47. Kural 595.
48. Kural 623.
49. Kural 596.
50. Sir Vidiadhar Surajprasad Naipaul is winner of the Nobel Prize in literature 2001. His writings dealt with the cultural confusion of the Third World.
51. Launched on 19 April, 1975.
52. Galileo Galilee lived in Italy during 1564-1642.
53. Abu Bakr As-Siddiq (The Upright) was the first Muslim caliph (632-634 AD).
54. The Kings of Persia (224-651 AD).
55. The Greek-speaking Roman Empire during the Middle Ages.
56. *Ja na koi hindu hai, Na ko musalaman* (Janam Sakhi).
57. Every tour is called 'Udasi'.
58. *Sacho urai sabh ko, opar sach achar.*
59. Holy Guru Granth Sahib, Jup 4: 187.
60. Famous for his thoughtful narrative of ten ideals that have shaped American thought, life, and the unique national identity.
61. American historian lived during 1899-1978.
62. Professor Emeritus of Mechanical Engineering and History at the University of Houston.
63. A world conflict occurring from 1914 to 1918.
64. Published on 20 August, 1862.
65. John Hope Franklin in *From Slavery to Freedom*.
66. For translated version of his cycle of song-poems, *Gitanjali*.
67. Harijan, 20-7-1935; Gandhian Institute Bombay Sarvodaya Mandal.

68. American journalist invited by Gandhiji in 1942; lived during 1896-1970.
69. Sri Eknath Easwaran is regarded as a great contemporary spiritual teacher.
70. Received Noble Prize in Literature 1990 for writing characterised by sensuous intelligence and humanistic integrity. Lived during 1914-1998; Mexican Ambassador in India during 1962-1968.
71. Einstein's letter to Gandhi written in 1931; Gandhi Serve Foundation.
72. Robert Kanigel is Professor of Science Writing at Massachusetts Institute of Technology.
73. Jai Maharaj, February 1990.
74. *The Giant Who Touched Tomorrow,* Tata Sons Ltd., 2005.
75. Defence Research & Development Organisation, New Delhi.
76. For his work on the scattering of light and for the discovery of the effect named after him.
77. Vinayak Bhat.
78. One of the world's oldest and richest musical traditions, Carnatic music is the classical music of Southern India. The basic form is a monophonic song with improvised variations.
79. Alexis Carrel (1873-1944) was mainly concerned with experimental surgery and the transplantation of tissues and whole organs. In 1912, he won the Nobel Prize in Medicine.
80. As a staff reporter for *The Wall Street Journal* Steven Mufson witnessed much of the 1984-1986 black uprising.
81. A British journalist, Anthony Terrell Seward Sampson (1926-2004) was a personal friend of Nelson Mandela.
82. Andre Brink is a White South African novelist whose anti-apartheid books inspired Nelson Mandela.

83. Address by President Nelson Mandela at Midrand on 10 October, 1998.
84. American essayist and poet (1803-1882).
85. Kural 157.
86. Volume 19 – Issue 02, Jan. 19 – Feb. 01, 2002.
87. *Current Science* 82: 222-225.
88. University was founded in 1925.
89. A Swedish, Dag Hjalmar Agne Carl Hammarskjöld (1905-1961) was elected Secretary-General of the United Nations in 1953 for a five-year term and re-elected in 1957.
90. English-born poet Wystan Hugh Auden (1907-1973) is widely considered among the greatest literary figures of the 20th century. "Beware of words, for with words we lie."
91. Amrita Patel, Chairman, National Dairy Development Board, Anand.
92. A central figure in the Mexican Green Revolution; Recipient of The Nobel Peace Prize 1970.
93. Physicist-Philosopher. Founder Chief of Defence Research & Development Organisation (1948-1961).
94. Page 212.
95. C.N.R. Rao is the Linus Pauling Research Professor and Honorary President of Jawaharlal Nehru Centre for Advanced Scientific Research, Bangalore.
96. The essence of *dogness,* according to Plato, is at a whole level of being more real than an individual dog.
97. Page 70.
98. Sudden unpleasant situations automatically generates negative emotions, including primitive anger feelings and hostile or flight impulses, even before the person has time to think about what has happened or what to do about it.
99. Czech-born German-speaking writer whose posthumously published noveis express the alienation of modern man. Lived during 1883-1924.

100. K. Ramchand, then Director of Centre for Airborne Systems (CABS).
101. A dish like structure mounted on the aircraft body.
102. President Lincoln wrote this letter expressing condolences to Mrs. Bixby, a widow on 21 November 1864.
103. Jean-Jacques Rousseau (1712-1778). He is best known for his *Social Contract* philosophy that describes the relationship of man with society.
104. Discrete objects created in the mind out of an inseparable reality. A term used by A.H. Almaas.
105. Around 200,000 Pound Sterling.
106. Qaloo ainnaka laanta yoosufa qala ana yoosufu wahatha akhee qad manna Allahu AAalayna innahu man yattaqi wayasbir fainna Allaha la yudeeAAu ajra almuhsineena (Yusuf; Holy Quran :12.90)
107. As many as 22 policemen were burnt alive by a rampaging mob after the police fired on a procession of satyagrahis in Chauri Chaura near Gorakhpur on 4 February 1922.
108. Addressed to Walter S Rogers, Institute of Current World Affairs, New York; courtesy New India Digest.
109. English Poet, Essayist and Lecturer; currently Professor of English Literature and Religion, at Boston University.
110. Fihi Ma Fihi 17, quoted in: Helminski, Kabir (2000). The Rumi Collection. P.16.

□

ACKNOWLEDGEMENTS

First and foremost, I wish to express my gratitude to Most Respected Swami Parmarthananda of Ramakrishna Math, Ven. U. Gnanarathana Thero, Bhikkhu-in-charge, Maha Bodhi Society of India; His Holiness Most Rev. Marampudi Joji, Arch Bishop of Hyderabad; His Holiness Maulana Mufti Mohd. Mukarram Ahmed, Shahi Imam, Masjid Fatehpuri, Delhi and Sardar Paramjit Singh Sarna, President, Delhi Sikh Gurudwara Prabandhak Committee for their blessings and guidance in completing this work which most certainly was beyond my capabilities to handle.

I owe a great debt of gratitude to B. Soma Raju, Chairman, CARE Hospital and my mentor for many years. He enthusiastically endorsed the book from its very beginning. With his trademark grace and thoughtfulness, he has provided me lot of reading material, all the freedom to travel and work on this book.

Syed Abdul Sayeed of Aligarh Muslim University and Y. Satyanarayana, Anwar-ul-Uloom College, Osmania University have provided the pillars of scholarship on which this book stands.

My sincere thanks to R. Swaminathan, my enligtened guide for the last two decades and S.M. Khan,

Press Secretary to the President of India, for sharing with me their wisdom and exchanging views with the kind of respect to my scholarship which I am not quite sure it deserves.

H. Sheridon and R.K. Prasad always looked after me whenever I was in Delhi, offered valuable assistance in my work. Sheridon has been a low key, considerate, and steadfast advocate of my books. I treasure his forthright friendship and cherish our time together at South Block, Vigyan Bhavan and in Rashtrapati Bhavan. I've come to rely heavily on his unimpeachable sensibilities.

P.S.R. Swami read numerous drafts of the book. Always cheerful and insightful, Swami offered critiques that proved to be indispensable. Dennis Marcus Mathew read through the final manuscript and very kindly provided valuable suggestions.

P. Krishnam Raju, Chairman, CARE Foundation, was first to read a rough draft and the last to put his stamp of approval on it. He was parsimonious in his praise and compassionate when he had to give me bad news. S.G. Prasad, my colleague, had been a great support to all my activities for the last several years. None of my work is complete without his participation including this book.

Anjana Tiwari, my wife, was indispensable to this work right from the very beginning. For more than 25 years, she has selflessly embraced all my endeavours, grounded or otherwise. So generously she shared my destiny.

Arun K. Tiwari

BIBLIOGRAPHY

Abdul Kalam, A.P.J. with Arun K. Tiwari—*Wings of Fire*, University Press, 1999.

Abdul Kalam, A.P.J.—*Ignited Minds: Unleashing the Power Within India*, Penguin, 2002.

Almaas, A.H.—*Inner Journey Home: The Soul's Realization of the Unity of Reality*, Shambhala, 2004.

Arthur Osborne (Editor)—*The Collected Works of Ramana Maharshi*, Weiser Books, 1997.

Auden, W.H. and Leif Sjoberg (Translator)—*Markings by Dag Hammarskjold*, Faber, 1964.

Baldwin, Neil—*Edison: Inventing the Century*, University of Chicago Press, 2001.

Bühler, G. (Translator)—*The Laws of Manu* In *The Sacred Books of the East, vol. 25*, Motilal Banarasidass, 1975.

Carrel, Alexis—*Man, The Unknown*, Macfadden, 1961.

Chesterton, G.K.—*Saint Francis of Assissi*, Random House, 2001.

Coleman, Barks—*Essential Rumi*, Harper, San Francisco, 1997.

Derek A. Long—*The Raman Effect : A Unified Treatment of the Theory of Raman Scattering by Molecules*, John Wiley & Sons, 2001.

Eknath Easwaran—*Gandhi, The Man: The Story of His Transformation*, Nilgiri Press (third edition), 1997.

Fischer, Louis—*Gandhi: His Life and Message for the World*, Signet Book, 1989.

Franklin, J.H.—*From Slavery to Freedom*, Alfred A. Knopf, 1988.

Franz Kafka and Harold Bloom (Editor)—*The Metamorphosis (Bloom's Modern Critical Interpretations)*, Chelsea House Publications, 1988.

Helminsky, Camille and Kabir—*Rumi: The Path of Love by Manuela Dunn Mascetti (Editor)*, Element Books, 1999.

Hill, Napoleon—*The Law of Success*, Master Mind Books, 2002.

James Allen—*As A Man Thinketh*, Peter Pauper Press, 1960.

James Joyce—*Portable James Joyce*, Penguin Books, 1976.

Josephson, Matthew—*Edison: A Biography*, History Book Club, 2003.

Jung, Carl G.—*Man and His Symbols*, Dell Publishing, 1968.

Kak, Subhash—*The Prajna Sutra*, Louisiana State University, Baton Rouge, 2003.

Kamath, M.V.—*Milkman from Anand: The Story of Verghese Kurien*, Konark Publishers, 1996.

Krishnamurti, Jiddu—*The First and Last Freedom*, Harper, 1975.

Kurien Verghese—*An Unfinished Dream*, Tata-McGraw-Hill, 1997.

Lienhard, John H.—*The Engines of Our Ingenuity: An Engineer Looks at Technology and Culture*, Oxford University Press. 2001.

Mandela, Nelson—*Long Walk to Freedom*, Back Bay Books, 1995.

Mufson, Steven—*Fighting Years: Black Resistance and the Struggle for a New South Africa*, Beacon Press, 1990.

Paz, Octavo— *In Light of India*, Rupa Paperback, 1998.

Price, Robert M.—*The Apartheid State in Crisis: Political Transformation in South Africa, 1975-1990*, Oxford University Press, 1991.

Radhakrishnan, S.—*Living with a Purpose*, Orient Paperbacks, 1977.

Row, Jaya—*Profile of the Perfect Person: Based on Bhagvad Gita Chapter II*, Jaico, 2004.

Sampson, Anthony—*Mandela : The Authorized Biography*, Knopf, 1999.

Solomon, Robert C. and Higgins, Kathleen (Editor)—*Reading Nietzsche*, Oxford University Press, 1990.

Subbarao, Kakarla with Arun K. Tiwari—*A Doctor's Story of Life and Death*, Ocean Books, 2002.

Thomas Byrom (Translator)—*The Heart of Awareness : A Translation of the Ashtavakra Gita*, Shambhala, 2001.

Venkataraman, G.—*Journey Into Light: Life and Science of C.V. Raman*, Indian Academy of Sciences, 1988.

□

INDEX

Ambedkar, Baba Sahib 70, 71
Anand, B. 120
Aryabhata 55-57
Ashiamma 80
Ashtavakra 6, 14, 162
Asoka 47-49, 111, 116
Aurelius, Marcus 30

Bhabha, Homi J. 94, 104,
Bhatnagar, R. Sqn Ldr 124
Borlaug, Norman E. 103
Bose, Jagdish Chandra 72
Brahm Prakash 94
Buddha 6, 75

Carrel, Alexis 87, 159
Chandrasekhar, Subrahmanyan 72
Confucius 30, 75

Dhawan, Satish 78, 94-99, 112

Edison, Thomas 62-64, 112, 160
Einstein, Albert 57, 70, 75, 100, 101, 116
Emerson, Ralph Waldo 93

Galileo 55
Gandhiji 64-71, 88, 90, 112, 113, 117, 137, 138
Girija, Jyothirllata 143
Gulzar 9
Guru Nanak 60, 61

Hameed Ali, A. 17, 18
Hill, Napoleon 38, 160

Ilango, P. 124

Jainulabdeen 38, 80, 85
Jayakumar, I. 124
Joyce, James 113, 160

Kak, Subhash 9, 160
Kothari, D.S. 94, 104
Krishnamurti, J. 120, 161
Kurien, Verghese 102-104, 111, 112, 116, 161

Lama, Dalai 70
Lincoln, Abraham 64, 65, 112, 125

Mahaprajna, Acharya 16
Mandela, Nelson 88-93, 112, 161
Martin Luther King Jr. 70
Mediratta, O.P. 97

Naipaul, Sir V.S. 53
Narasimha, Roddam 95, 96
Narasimhaswamy, D. 124
Nietzsche 16, 161

Paz, Octavo 69, 70, 161
Ping, Ji 23
Prasad, B.N. 114
Pythagoras 43-55

Radhakrishnan, S. 41, 140, 161
Rajan, Y.S. 143
Raju, B. Soma 114, 157
Ramachandran, R. 94
Raman, C.V. 72, 75-79, 113, 160, 162
Ramana, Maharshi 15, 159
Ramanna, Raja 94, 101
Ramanujan, S. 72-74, 112, 118
Ramchand, K. 123, 124
Rao, C.N.R. 108
Ravi, S. Sqn Ldr 124
Rumi, Jalaluddin 11, 43, 146

Saha, Meghnath 72
Sarabhai, Vikram 94, 98, 104
Seshu, N.V. Sqn Ldr 124
Shaju, K.P. 124
Singh, Haridwar 131-133
Socrates 75
St. Francis 35
Subbarao, Kakarla 105-107, 111, 112, 162
Subbulakshmi, M.S. 86, 87, 118

Tagore, Rabindranath 66
Tata, Jamsetji 74, 75
Thiruvalluvar 49-52, 54, 93
Tipnis, Air Chief Marshal A.Y. 124
Tzu, Meng 23

Umar, Caliph 57-59, 112, 117, 118

Venkataraman, G. 76, 77, 162
Venkataraman, P. Sqn Ldr 124
Visvesvaraya, M. 72
Vivekananda 74, 75

□□□